P O E M S.

BY

WILLIAM H. HOLCOMBE, M.D.

NEW YORK:
MASON BROTHERS,
5 & 7 MERCER STREET

1860.

STEREOTYPED BY
SMITH & McDOUGAL,
84 Beekman-st., N. Y.

PRINTED BY
C. A. ALVORD,
15 Vandewater-st.

TO

MY BROTHER,

JAMES P. HOLCOMBE, L.L.D.,

PROFESSOR OF CIVIL, CONSTITUTIONAL AND INTERNATIONAL LAW, IN THE UNIVERSITY OF VIRGINIA,

BY WHOSE FRATERNAL SOLICITUDE AND EXAMPLE

MY LOVE OF LITERATURE WAS FIRST ENKINDLED,

This Little Volume

IS MOST AFFECTIONATELY INSCRIBED.

PREFACE.

THE pursuit of Literature has been with me, not a business, but an occasional recreation. Assiduous devotion to the Medical Profession for the last fifteen years has left me little time or inclination to cultivate the Poetic Art. Still, the material for a small volume has gradually accumulated, and with diffidence I make my first, and most probably my last contribution to the stock of American Poetry.

Several of the pieces are based upon the beautiful psychological doctrines of Swedenborg; and for the benefit of those who are unacquainted with his writings, I have appended, in the form of notes, some interesting extracts from his works, elucidative of the subject-matter of the poems.

Whilst I am not indifferent as to the verdict which the critics and time will pass upon these effusions, I have published them for the purpose, as Mrs. Browning expresses it, "of throwing them behind me, so as to leave clear the path before, toward better aims and ends."

May, 1869.

CONTENTS.

PAGE

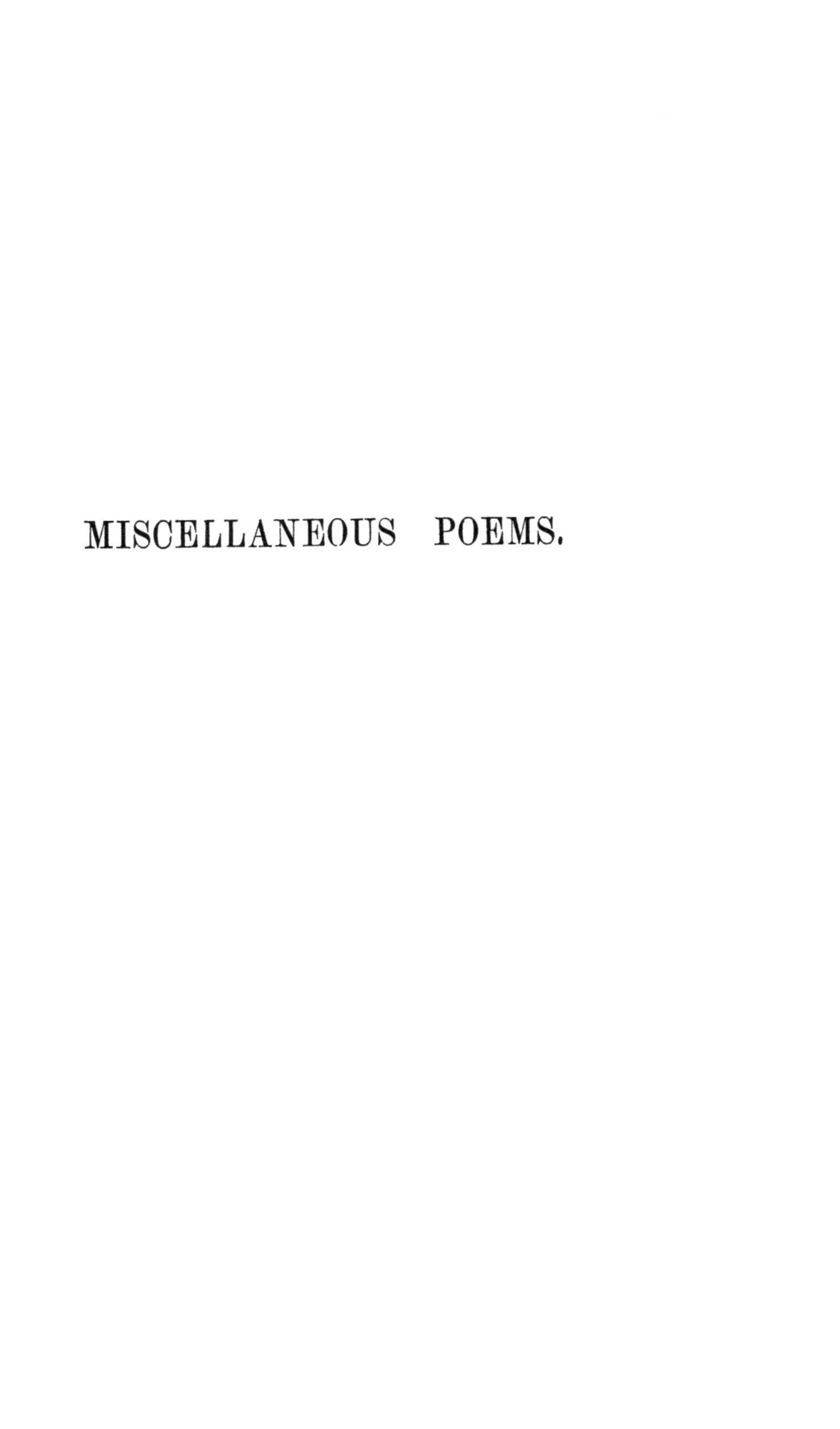

MISCELLANEOUS POEMS.

ODE

ON THE BIRTH OF A CHILD.

I.

A CHILD is born!
The joyous tidings sent
Go leaping jubilant
From tongue to tongue in music on,
A child is born!
Rejoice, thou mighty Human Heart!
Another fountain from the sacred ocean
Begins on earth its individual motion;
Another life from God's life flows apart
And feels the throb of its identity.
Self-conscious, loving, knowing, seeing,
Time-thralled and yet eternal being,
Thou heaven-derived humanity!

How holy is thy birth!
Some star our sense discovers not
Enunciative points the spot,
And angel-choirs are chanting here
To guardian spirits kneeling near,
"Glory to God and peace on earth!"

II.

O Man! Thou art the heart of nature!
Thy pulses pass to every creature;
The electric motions of thy soul
Through all the living kingdoms roll,
Flow to the earth and animate the whole.
For this bright being which before us lies,
The world is full of innate sympathies.
The trees rejoice as when a bud
Peeps crimson from its mother-wood;
From nest to nest successive springs
A choral twitter of delight,
As if some pair of little wings
Were spread for their initial flight;

The rivulets lisp the tidings on,
Rippling it out to moss and stone;
Flower winks to flower with smiling nod,
And morning, on the hills aglow,
Bids all her tip-toe breezes blow
To waft the message, come from God—
A child is born! a sign is given!
A living revelation made from heaven!

III.

This Human Soul,
This flesh-engirdled flame,
This microcosm of the whole!
What seer's or sage's erudition
Can satisfy the child's petition,
And tell us whence, and how, and why it came?
Not in this present sensuous sphere
Hath this mysterious life begun:
The meanest flower that blossoms here
Was once an essence in the sun;
And naught of nature's dead material
Is woven into our woof ethereal.

Through inner realms of light
This star descended by a path unknown,
Invisible in its superior zone
Until it burst, thus beautiful and bright,
Upon our happy sight.
Yet hath it tokens of its derivation.
There is no wave without some agitation,
No subtlest ether without some vibration:
All things have traces which reveal
What they have felt or what they feel.
The shell-fish tints his convoluted chamber
With his own hues of purple, pearl and amber;
The rose's leaf betrays impresses
Where fairy lips have left caresses;
And this sweet face, so round and small,
Index of scarcely aught at all,
Hath delicate motions not its own,
Dimples like shadows o'er it thrown,
The last, faint, trembling terminations
Of wonderful irradiations
From angel-presences within,
And those Eternal Powers to which we are akin.

IV.

O infancy! with all thy forms enchanting,
Thou art the nursery of paradise;
Whither the Master frequent comes, transplanting
Some favorite to His mansions in the skies.
The little graves we water with our tears
Are naught but empty sepulchers,
Whence the dear souls, unbound, unladen,
Have risen to their eternal Eden.
Under the Saviour's merciful direction
Still are they linked by innermost affection,
More durable than blood or birth,
To kindred spirits left on earth;
Like zephyrs which are the souls of flowers
Released by time's cold touch or ours;
Returning with most melodious motions,
With sweet invisible devotions,
Dallying about their sister-blossoms,
Breathing their lives into their bosoms!

V.

O see! a morn of May!
A shining, balmy, breezy one;
The little children out at play
On sweet, green landscapes in the sun:
Searching for shells the rivulet's brim,
Watching the silver minnows swim,
Chasing the rainbow butterfly,
Or mocking echo's faint reply.
O trustful, happy, guileless creatures!
How near ye are to angel-natures!
Content with what each day is given
And fed with manna fresh from heaven.
The little loves and charities,
The sweet and gentle courtesies
Ye from each other thus evoke at play,
Are treasures inly stored away.
Into their forms, like dew into the flower
The Lord distills his vivifying power,
And blessings they become for ever;
States of the mind which perish never;

But losing every tint of sadness
Return with multiplying gladness;
Germs of eternal happiness
Which never cease to grow and bless;
Strength for the seasons of temptation,
Means of eventual renovation,
The bonds that link us to the angels most—
The light which may be hidden, but never can be lost!

VI.

The Golden Age so full of love and grace
Was but the sunny childhood of our race;
And its bright angels from the inmost heaven
As guardian-spirits to our babes are given.
Thus childhood with its sweet conditions,
Its pure, angelic intuitions,
Its gentle, untaught sympathies,
And all its dear credulities,
Is a bright record which may prove
To skeptic sensualists extreme
The possibility of love,
And old traditions not a dream.
It is a symbol of our primal glory,
The sweet-toned echo of its wondrous story;

A fragment beautiful and ample,
A column of the buried temple.
Yet are these vestiges of daylight gone,
Purplings prophetic of another sun,
Beneath whose glorious illustration
Shall come the promised restoration
From sin and grief and pain ;
When Man shall be a Child again !
And in whose light, more plastic far than ours,
The angels of the highest heaven appear
To those who view them from an humbler sphere
As naked infants garlanded with flowers.

OUR LITTLE ALECK.

WHEN thou wert born, my angel boy!
  I wrote a song for thee;
The music of that wondrous joy
  Which thou wert then to me.

Alas! alas! the tribute lay,
  My heart so fondly gave,
In requiem echoes died away
  Upon thy little grave.

Soon, soon the fountains which supplied
  Thy precious wants went dry,
But sorrow's never-ebbing tide
  Yet fills thy mother's eye.

Mute her guitar's untended strings,
  Her book lies on the shelf;
She weeps o'er all thy little things
  As if they were thyself;

As if they were that beauteous form
  We left in earth alone,
The little cage whence bright and warm
  The heavenly bird had flown.

O Aleck! since thy little star
  Hath vanished into heaven,
All earthly things have seemed ajar,
  And—may we be forgiven

If it is sinful! but we crave
  What Heaven will surely give,
Death with thy body in the grave
  And life where thou dost live.

THE LOST TREASURE.

Oft in the sunny Spring
When pretty buds are peeping,
Sad are the thoughts they bring,
How can we cease from weeping?
Our own sweet Bud,
So pure and good,
In which our hearts delighted,
The spoiler's breath,
The frost of Death,
Our own sweet Bud has blighted.
So, in the sunny Spring,
When pretty buds are peeping,
Sad are the thoughts they bring,
How can we cease from weeping?

Oft on the Summer morns,
  When azure birds are flying,
Our hearts amid their thorns
  Are sighing, ever sighing.
        Our own sweet Bird
        No more is heard,
    Its heavenly flight is taken!
        Its light is gone,
        Its music flown,
    And we are left forsaken!
So, on the Summer morns,
  When azure birds are flying,
Our hearts amid their thorns,
  Are sighing, ever sighing.

Oft on the Autumn days,
  When blight is all-pervading,
We smile with thankful praise
  That Life itself is fading.
        How glad and free,
        O! we shall be
    To drop its heavy burden!

Our Bud shall spring,
Our Bird shall sing
Again, beyond the Jordan!
So, in the Autumn days,
When blight is all-pervading,
We smile with thankful praise
That Life itself is fading.

OUR THREE CHILDREN.

WITH three sweet children are we blest!
  Aleck we feel but cannot see;
Warwick is at his mother's breast,
  And Lucy on her father's knee;
Five forms, united, yet apart—
Five faces and a single heart.

Aleck, the happiest, passed away
  Softly as sunset into heaven,
A seraph-child, on earth astray,
  And back to seeking Seraphs given;
But casting on us from above
His double image for our love.

We need no little sepulcher
  Where roses and sweet-williams grow,

No little garments kept with care,
  No little playthings—treasured so!
We need no tokens of such kind
To keep our angel-boy in mind.

He comes in Lucy's shining face
  And in her ringlets, strand for strand,
His little gestures, full of grace,
  Are made with Warwick's dimpled hand;
Through Lucy's lips we hear him speak,
We kiss his tears from Warwick's cheek.

Our Aleck is a little star
  That leads our hearts to Bethlehem,
With angel-voices from afar.
  Jesus, our Lord! we follow them;
We bring to Thee with faith intense
Our gold, our myrrh, our frankincense!

THE ANGEL OF MORNING.

I cannot discover my face to your sight,
  Nor tell you the name which in heaven I bear:
That face would dissolve into haloes of light,
  The name into musical tones on the air.

But, breathing the life of an age which has gone,
  You may call me Aurora, the far-shining one,
Who dwells in the shell-tinctured tent of the morn,
  And sits like a page at the feet of the sun.

I watch o'er the beautiful souls who begin
  The morning of life undefaced by a stain,
And o'er those who awake from the dark night
    of sin
  To the spiritual morning, like children again.

IS THIS THE SPOT?

Is this the spot where once so well
  My taskless childhood loved to stray?
Where now the sweet but nameless spell
  Which lured mine idle step away?

The charms which then my fancy fed
  In vain I now essay to find,
The Spirit of the place has fled
  And left its grosser part behind.

The rocks are not so quaint and gray,
  The leaves are not so fresh and green;
The brook upon its noisy way
  Is cheerless through the sylvan scene.

I am not raptured now to hear
  The warbled joys from every bough ;
The witching sky, so blue and clear,
  Is but a common prospect now.

'Tis I have changed ! for nature still
  To childhood's heart is just as dear,
And forests, waters, field and hill
  Have music for its listening ear.

The dream of youth, which comes to all,
  Has passed like bright Aurora's train ;
Sweet Memory may its form recall,
  But cannot give its power again.

The silvery streamlet of the glen,
  Which loves and fairies hovered o'er,
Has flowed into the haunts of men
  And lost its beauties evermore.

CHILDHOOD.

O SCENES of my Childhood! ye cannot restore me
  The light and the glow of my life's early dawn;
The gardens, the meadows, the hills are before me,
  But something which gave them their glory has
      gone.

The roses are blooming by zephyr still haunted,
  And evening all dreamily sits by the stream;
But ah! not the roses my sweet mother planted,
  And ah! not the evening when love was the
      dream!

Like skies in the depth of a bright lake inverted,
  Heaven lies in the heart of our childhood serene;
But dark as that water by sunlight deserted
  Is the spirit where Time with its shadow hath
      been.

The best of the Angels who love us and guide us
  Attend upon Childhood and gladden its way;
But subtly the Demons of evil divide us
  And lead the young flocks from their shepherds
      astray.

Though far from their care, and in spite of their
      warning
  We wander away on a sorrowful track,
Those Angels of youth, on the hills of the morning,
  Stand star-like in glory and beckon us back.

Their eyes still pursue us with radiant affection,
  They sigh that our life from their own is with-
      drawn,
We feel their regrets, and with fond recollection
  We sigh in return that our childhood has gone.

TO MY MOTHER.

No fresh green spot of Spring is found,
The wintry snow has clad the ground,
The cold air has no joyful sound,
My mother!

Hushed is the water's note of glee,
No song comes from the birdless tree,
But yet I have a song for thee,
My mother!

For till the light of love depart,
There is a spring within my heart
Of which the changeless sun thou art,
My mother!

When childhood welcomed bird and bee,
When music breathed from every tree,
When thou wert all in all to me,
My mother!

When nature's sunlight on my brow
Was not so tinged with shade as now,
And all things seemed as kind as thou,
My mother!

My view of life was like a scene
Deep-mirrored in a lake serene,
Bright, loving skies and hills of green,
My mother!

The picture now is not so fair,
For winds of doubt and clouds of care
Have broke the glittering calmness there,
My mother!

But still the memory of thy face
All later memories can replace,
The winds can calm—the clouds can chase—
My mother!

And to the spirit sorrow-riven
Restore that light so early given,
The light that leads—with thee—to heaven,
My mother!

THE FIRST FLOWER.

O BEAUTIFUL and glorious birth!
  We bless thee, child-like one!
Born of our sacred mother Earth
  And fathered by the Sun.

Hail! sweet and solitary Flower!
  Like the first star above,
That comes before his evening hour
  As on a work of love;

Like the first faint and tender light
  The crescent moon displays;
Like the first touch of ether bright
  Before the morning's blaze;

Like the first pleasant woodland sound
  The Southern warblers bring,
Which follow o'er the greening ground
  The dewy step of Spring.

Evening has now a gentler beam,
  And Morn a brighter glow;
While mountain summits give the stream
  Their fast dissolving snow.

Thus, from the varied mental year
  May wintry sorrows flee!
And the first bud of Joy appear,
  O beauteous Flower, with thee!

RECOLLECTIONS OF THE BLUE RIDGE.

Thou dearest Mountain of the range!
  At whose eternal base I drew
My breath, and where I would exchange
  Earth's light for heaven's unfolding view;

My sensuous body stands afar,
  An alien form in toil and pain;
My Spirit, leaping like a star,
  Looks from thy sunny side again.

Beneath the glow of summer day
  Thy linkéd sisters sweetly lie,
Stretching their soft blue arms away,
  Almost incorporate with the sky.

One bird, like single ship at sea,
  Swims on the shining air alone;
The rivulet, like a child astray,
  Weeps o'er its couch of mountain stone.

The wind sighs gently through the pine
  With that ethereal sound which stirs,
In soft responsive hearts like mine,
  Thoughts that are symboled best by tears.

Down, down the valley, glimmering far,
  My native town, embowered in trees,
Sends up its household smoke in air
  To melt into the passing breeze.

While casual from the forest green
  Beams out old James's sparkling crest;
Where oft in boyhood I have seen
  His silver roll of morning mist.

And yonder is the sacred ground
  Where many a friend and kinsman lies;
The sun, from many a marbled mound,
  Glints brightly to my moistened eyes.

Alas! the scene, so sweet and fair,
  Fades like dissolving fairy spell;
A spectral twilight films the air,
  And dirges break from memory's bell!

MY LITTLE NED AND I.

My little playmate 's dead and gone!
  I gave him many a tear!
A merry little negro boy,
  Just twelve years old this year.
Alas! that on my childhood's heart
  So great a grief should lie!
We 'll no more play, by night or day,
  My little Ned and I!

He was my shadow where I went,
  Subservient to my will,
But with enduring gentleness
  He made me gentler still.
We climb'd the trees, we bridged the brook,
  We chased the butterfly;
We 'll no more play, by night or day,
  My little Ned and I!

I knew, when he became so ill,
  His little soul would go,
Although my mother nursed him well,
  And the doctor said, "Oh no!"
For I had dreamed I saw his face
  Look smiling from the sky;
We'll no more play, by night or day,
  My little Ned and I!

I heard him talking to himself
  About the children fair,
With spangled dresses, all so fine,
  Who played around him there;
He whispered low and promised them
  To join them by and by;
We'll no more play, by night or day,
  My little Ned and I!

That long, long night we watched his death,
  The dogs howled at the door,
The owls cried from the forest tree
  A hundred times or more;
My mother closed his glazing eyes,
  Whilst I stood sobbing by;

We 'll no more play, by night or day,
  My little Ned and I!

And when the great plantation bell
  Resounded for the roll,
The roll-call of the heavens received
  Another shining soul.
I am a schoolboy now—and he—
  An angel in the sky;
We 'll no more play, by night or day,
  My little Ned and I!

THE STRAY LAMB.

WHAT dost thou, timid creature! here,
In mute astonishment and fear,
Gazing so meekly up and down
The crowded avenues of town?
While at some window, far away,
Regardless now of books or play,
Thy little mistress sits forlorn,
Disconsolate since thou hast gone;
Like a poor mother, full of fears,
Weeping and watching through her tears;
Weeping for one allured to roam
From all the sanctities of home,

And wander down life's devious way,
From duty, love and peace astray,
Watching, with each returning sun,
For him—the unreturning one.

Poor truant nursling of the fold!
Bewildered, lonely, sad and cold,
Remote from thy congenial sphere,
Unloved, unled, unpitied here,
Dost thou not gaze far down the street,
Where woods and skies in vista meet—
The woods of greenest, fairest hue,
The skies of brightest, loving blue—
And fancy what awaits thee there?
A life serene, a lustrous air,
A shaded, quiet, cool retreat,
A haven from the dust and heat,
With longings such as poet feels
For what his inward sense reveals,
With visions such as mortals have
Of life and rest beyond the grave.

Lives there a man could pass thee by
With busy step and heedless eye,

Nor through the veil of seeming chance
Discern thy true significance?
A still small voice I deem thou art,
A brief, bright moral to the heart;
One of those lessons round us strown
In sounds and colors, leaf and stone,
Whereby consoling angels can
Converse in symbols still with man;
Such as a violet's modest face
Illumining some desert place,
A single star, whose eye of light
Peers underneath some cloud of night;
A smile of resignation meek,
Sparkling on sorrow's furrowed cheek;
A child's dear shout of merriment,
A wild bird's carol of content,
Bursting upon us unawares,
When we are burdened down with cares;
Melodious memories unsought,
Startling us into pleasant thought;
Things of an evanescent power
Brief as the fragrance of a flower,
Which, having been, may be no more,
But leave us better than before.

There is not in this world of sin
A soul so deeply sunk therein,
Thronged though it be with crimes and cares,
Revenges, malices, despairs ;
However dire the phantoms there,
However pestilent its air,
However dreary its abodes,
And dedicate to demon-gods,
But in its thoroughfares, night and day,
There ever is some Lamb astray,
Some light from heaven, some fragment thence
Of primal love and innocence,
Which keeps the angels on its track
To lead, and love, and lure it back !

LITTLE JULE.

Little Jule at yonder sod
  Weeps as if her heart would break;
In the graveyard, newly trod,
  Weeps for little Lucy's sake!
    Angel Lucy! sweet and mild,
    Scarce a baby, scarce a child:
    Slowly, softly laid away
    Underneath the fearful clay;
    Kisses on her little brow,
    Ah! she does not feel them now!
    Roses on her little bosom,
    Her sweet self a broken blossom!
Now the ladies turn away
  With their weeping almost blind;
Little Jule in twilight gray
  Lingers weeping still behind.

Little slave! why shouldst thou care
  Thus thy foolish heart to break;
Weeping solitary here
  For this little Lucy's sake?
    O the world is cold and lone!
    Little mistress dead and gone!
    Little playthings put away,
    Things for tears and not for play;
    Little cradle, rocked no more,
    All the little prattling o'er!
    Every little pout forgot,
    And a frown remembered not,
    Every little kiss and word
    Doubly, trebly, now endeared.—
Let her watch and let her weep
  At the little new-made grave!
Sacred watch will Angels keep
  O'er the mistress and the slave!

ROSEBUD AND SUNBEAM.

A Rosebud unfolded its leaves to the view,
All crimson with beauty, all brightened with dew,
Like a soul which has fallen from happier spheres,
Yet smiling with hope through its penitent tears.

A Sunbeam came down to the heart of the Rose,
Like a thought which illumines the mind where
it glows;
Like an angel come down from the bright world
of bliss
To commune with some beautiful spirit in this.

When homeward the Sunbeam retreated at even,
The soul of the Flower went as fragrance to heaven,
As the heart which has cherished some Truth from
above,
Ascends with that Truth to the regions of Love.

SUBSTANCE AND SHADOW,

OR, THE CHILD AND THE RIVULET.

I see a bright and joyous Child astray
Along the Brooklet in a vernal meadow;
I watch their gentle harmonies at play,
As one might watch a violet and its shadow.

Is not the Rivulet's verdure, sweet and wild,
Symbol of something in the living creature?
The thoughts and loves and raptures of the Child
In flower-forms imaged on the face of nature?

Those sounds which make the listener's heart rejoice,
Those jubilant notes upon the ether flying,
Have in the rippling Stream an answering Voice
Like their own echoes from the earth replying.

Those smiles of innocent beauty, sign and seal
  Of angel-presence in the young affection,
Are like these sheeny sparkles which reveal
  The loving sun in thousand-fold reflection.

From ancient hills beneath auroral beam
  Crept out the Brook with dewy kisses laden,
Pure, bright and silent, like the human Stream,
  Forth-stealing from the golden gates of Eden.

Unvexed, unviolated, free they roam,
  Those mated currents gloriously outflowing,
The light and music of their little home,
  Receiving joy and double joy bestowing.

Each in its sphere of action onward pours,
  Lapsing away from early bird and blossom,
Till strange creations rise upon its shores,
  And mighty shadows sink into its bosom.

The human channel wears into the grave,
  Losing on earth its individual motion,
While its bright symbol, the complying Wave,
  Gives up its being to the wasteful ocean.

But lo! the halcyon vision re-appears!
  An Angel stands beside the Crystal River!
The heart of Childhood in celestial spheres
  Is pictured in the Stream of Life forever!

Truth lies concealed within this metaphor;
  Substance is dual in its every feature;
Our Souls are mirrored all around us here,
  Our lives repeated in the forms of Nature.

THE INVISIBLE.

I 've heard sweet bells upon the breeze
  When none were ringing,
And the soft sound of waving trees,
  And insect-singing.

Though in the woodland, still and deep,
  No leaf was falling,
And e'en the clouds were laid asleep.
  They were Spirits calling :

Voices they were with whisperings
  Of friends departed ;
Angels they were with comfortings
  For the weary-hearted.

THE PICTURE.

I SAW a lovely Picture
  In a gallery of Art,
Which charmed me like an April rose,
  And I wear it in my heart;
Not like the rose of gardens,
  Which withers soon away,
But planted in my heart of hearts,
  It never shall decay.

It was a blooming Maiden,
  So beautiful and pure,
T' was mirrored from an angel's face
  In a vision, I am sure.

A Dove of heavenly plumage
  Upon her bosom lay;
I saw the Spirit of the Dove
  Around her lips at play.

I longed to see the Painter,
  I longed to grasp his hand,
I know there is a common ground
  Whereon we two could stand.
I know he has been happy,
  And his heart is full of love,
Or he never could have imaged forth
  That Maiden and her Dove.

For as the Dove resembles
  The Virgin's spotless thought,
So is this Picture like the Soul
  From which it was outwrought;
And of that glorious Spirit
  I catch a radiant part,
Which I have called a rose—and plant
  Forever in my heart.

RECOVERY FROM YELLOW FEVER.

Oh joy! the crisis comes! Earth bears me back
Triumphant from the fearful grasp of Night
Unto the myriad scenes of Life again.
The pleasant morn is shining in my face,
I hear the loud wind blowing in the trees,
Ah me! how musically! I behold
The clouds glide by my window on their far,
Deep journeys in the sky, and I would send
Praises and thanks, could they be messengers
Of aught emotional. Upon the fields,
Upon the woods, the waters, everywhere,
Sunlight has dropt his colors, and they lie
In bright and living beauty. What a world
Of wonders do I see, hear, feel again!

Late I was curtained from the happy round
Of day and night, and from all human things;
Pained, fevered, tortured, stupored by disease.
Death, who e'er stalks the garden of our life,
Gathering the withered blossoms to his hand,
Whilst the soul-essences exhale to heaven,
Surveyed me with fixed eye. Dire phantasy
Crowded the burning chambers of the brain
With frightful images. Tempests at sea,
Storms, heaving, blackening, roaring o'er the land,
Painful and difficult escapes from peril,
And all imaginable scenes of blood—
Staggering in flight, from fierce hyena howls,
O'er the hot sands of silent wildernesses—
From crag to crag, down to some unknown beach,
Interminably falling, falling, falling—
Or swimming, floating far away, forlorn,
In uproar of the elemental world—
Such were my dreams of horror. Sounds I heard
But not interpretable, and I saw
Gigantic shapes in threatening attitudes
Stalking athwart the murky air, which lay
Like a sea-mist betwixt me and the sun.

When the fierce morbid fires had paled away,
Left powerless, trembling on the sluggish verge
Of Lethe's ashen water, I beheld
A soft array of gentler, brighter scenes,
Yet touched with melancholy. The old brook
Whereby I spent my wild vacation hours,
With a loved playmate's sweet, alluring voice,
Called me to ramble with it down the glen,
Twirling the leaves and kissing all the flowers ;
But when I thought I reached its sparkling brim,
The voice went further down the dale, receding,
Which I pursued o'er rugged rocks, alone,
Till I despaired, for it receded still,
Smiling through trees and calling as it ran.
Then saw I Florence in the orchard walks
Float o'er the ground like music, bright as June,
Sporting with golden locks and childish joy
About the rose-red apples. And I went
Searching and sighing through the mellowed shade,
From path to path, from tree to tree, in pain,
Searching and sighing, for the fairy form
Had vanished like a sunbeam. Last I heard
Remote but clear a bell of strangest sound,
Ringing and ringing in a dark, green wood,

Such pure, sweet, melting, holy cadences,
That eagerly with tears I followed them,
But chased the flying echoes all in vain,
And stood in ancient solitudes of shade
Silent and wonder-riven, whilst overhead
Angels were whispering in the summer air.

As 'twere a river of life and human sense,
A gentle river ebbing to the sea,
Dripping away from lawn, and field, and bower,
From all that loved it and from all it loved,
Seemed my own soul when passing, as I thought,
From earth and all its dear ones. Sad I stood
At the dark gateway which divides our lives
Present and future. One sweet form was near,
Made mine in heaven and earth, whose angel face
Shone star-like round the darkness of my couch.
The rest were happy in Virginian homes.
Strangers would bury me and leave my grave
Unmarked, unvisited by friends or flowers.
Then, like a picture looming from afar,
I saw a little family of grief :
A noble, gray-haired, venerable man,
Bowed silently ; my kind old grandmother

Grieved in her corner at the common loss ;
My pale-faced mother praying through her tears ;
And a sad group of manly brothers, touched
Each his own way with sorrow. But they passed
Like shadows o'er my brain, and then came on
A crowd of undistinguishable thoughts,
Hopes, fears and wishes, but not unillumed
By calms of prayer and some few blissful gleams
Of Heaven's eternal city.

Author of Life ! from whom I have derived
This fresh, warm stream which quickens now my
spirit,
So let me keep it for my daily being,
So use it in Thy will—that without fear
And with the resignation of a heart
Made Thine entirely, I may give it back
At Thine own bidding !

THE MOUNTAIN HEIGHT.

Oh! for the bold and breezy height
  Of some old Alp or Appenine,
Waving with oak and laurel bright,
  Or cedar and the odorous pine;
  Radiantly colored with the shine
Of summer sun, and far above
  This dull and dusty atmosphere,
  Where man is racked with toil and care,
And little knows or feels of love!

Beneath the shadow of vast trees,
  On such a summit I could lie
All the bright afternoon at ease,
  And from the aerial station spy

The spread of valleys far and wide,
Sloping to hills on either side,
  Tinctured with sunlight and the gleams
Of clustered domes and rural homes,
  Of groves, green knolls, and glinting streams,
And all that makes life rich and sweet,
Brilliantly pictured at my feet:
  Till all things darkened from afar
And Twilight solemn, slow and late,
Came weeping from the western gate
  Of heaven and lit her single star.

Nor sad nor lonely I would note
  In the sweet hush of mountain air,
From all the life of man remote
  What glorious tides of life are there!
An insect world, with joy replete,
Would throb serenely at my feet;
The birds in every arbored nook
Be musical; the new-born brook,
From its rock-cradle peeping forth,
Would lisp the secret of its birth,
And stealing with a pleasant sheen
  Like infant-smile, from out the shade,

Fling careless down the deep ravine
 And shatter into white cascade :
A thing of motion, music, mirth !
 As if a rainbow, tempest-riven,
 Had melted from the walls of heaven
And made a rivulet on the earth.

And see ! on subtlest ether borne,
 The floating palaces of cloud !
Suburban villas of the sun,
Wrought by the winds in gorgeous mold,
With sapphire tissues, pearl and gold !
Behind whose transitory walls,
Sits Orion in his starry halls,
 Tuning his lyre for coming night,
Which those can almost hear who stand
 Upon the lustrous mountain height,
A promontory of the Land,
 Far-stretching in a Sea of Light.

SPIRITUAL FLOWERS.

In every human heart there grows
  A sister pair of fadeless flowers;
Truth is the Lily—Love the Rose—
  Transplanted from celestial bowers.

'T is watchful Duty's gentle care,
  To keep them ever in her sight;
To feed them on the beams of air,
  And shield them from the dews of night.

And when they've filled the little sphere
  To earthly joys and sorrows given,
Commissioned Angels will appear,
  And bear the exiles back to heaven.

TO A ROSE.

ABOUT thy form, O child of Spring,
The trilling blue-bird loves to sing,
And bees and winds and dews repair
To taste the breathing fragrance there;
But not thy beauties outward shown,
Are treasures to my heart alone:
For, radiant Rose! thou art to me
The pledge of things I can not see,
A Messenger, a Mystery.

O, were the lustrous fountain sought,
Sweet symbol of ethereal thought!
From whence thy stream of being sprung,
Outflowing thus so bright and young;

Methinks, O Rose! it would be found
A Fountain on celestial ground,
Whence God's divinest blessings flow,
Through spirit-realms to man below,
And duplicate on nature's face
The tokens of his power and grace.

Then, lovely Herald! linger long,
Like echo of an angel's song,
Like angel-thought from brighter sphere,
In beauty architectured here.
And when thy tissues fade and fall,
This moral shall my heart recall,
Our life is never lost when gone,
But life to deeper life withdrawn!

THE CHIMES.

THE stillness of the sunny Sabbath morn
Is broken by a chime of tuneful bells!
The strains of this aerial music come
Loud, long and cheerful, swelling forth in glee;
Then die complainingly upon the air,
And when you pause and list, and deem them gone,
Break out again in freshness and in joy.
Oft have I hearkened to the varying peal,
And fondly dreamed ("which was not all a dream")
That in the intonations there were couched
Expressions for each passion of the heart.

The soft and silver tone was that of *Hope*,
Stealing persuasively into the ear;
Such tone as I have thought the waters gave
When tinkling through the meadows of the Spring,

Or mated birds, in glow of mutual love,
Building their nests within a glittering tent
Of blended leaves and blossoms. Quick and shrill
As wild alarm of fire, or call to arms,
Fear's startled voice, but changing to *Despair*,
Its throbs tumultuous slowly softened down,
Through tolling bell and beat of muffled drum,
Down into breathless silence. Bursting forth
Without a discord was the note of *Joy*,
Full, rapid e'en to mirthfulness, like that
With which my childhood's heart leaped up to hear
My village church-bells, in the Sabbath sun,
Peal gaily forth. A melancholy voice,
Yet with a trace of Hope's melodious sound,
A gentle, pensive, beauteous symphony,
Dallying in fondness on the patient air,
I took for *Love's*, and treasured in my soul.
Too well I knew the fitful wail of *Grief!*
A plaintive song, such as the Autumn wind
Sings softly to itself in faded woods,
Seeking in vain the many-colored flowers
The Spring had promised. And my soul arose
Higher and higher, when *Triumphant Faith*,
Exultant o'er calamity and death,

Poured its condensed vibrations on the air,
Like the wild chanting of cathedral choirs,
Or the far-smiting thunder of the sea ;
Yea—almost imitative of that song
The morning angels, in their flaming robes,
Raise for the coming Sun.
When I have strayed
Too far on the entangled path of life,
And have forgotten Man's great destinies,
O, Sacred Herald ! call me sweetly back
By the pure influence of thy holy chime.
Wake once again that music of the mind,
When pleasing thoughts like pleasing sounds unite,
And melt me into reverential joy !

ODE TO POWERS' GREEK SLAVE.

Ideal of all hearts! what hast thou done,
    Thus fettered, silent, melancholy?
    Thou! beautiful, serene and holy,
As mountain summit hallowed by the Sun,
    Or Star dispensing sweetest light
    O'er the subdued and silent realm of night.
Can Beauty such as in thy form appears
Partake our common hopes and fears?
Feel human love or grieve with human tears?

In the serene and spiritual atmosphere
    From thy pure chastity outflowing,
    Around thee luminously glowing,
We do forget thy mortal grief and care;

And see thee by interior light,
A Revelation to our mental sight;
Thy Beauty with diviner meaning fraught,
A Shining Hieroglyph outwrought,
Ethereal vesture of Eternal Thought!

Thou art the entrancéd Spirit of our Race
Bowed in submissive meditation,
Silent in deep humiliation,
Unsphered and exiled from thy heavenly place;
In sin's austerest bondage now,
Yet with the light of Eden on thy brow,
A bow of promise, shining to reprove
Our hearts, incredulous of Love
And those sweet Powers which guide us from above.

We may not liken thee to earthly things;
To aught that might be changed or perish,
To aught that we could cease to cherish,
Bright outbirth of our best imaginings!
Thou Sunbeam of the spiritual sphere,
Caught from its ether and embodied here,

Making such music in our mental frame
As from the Egyptian statue came,
When the Sun touched it with his lips of flame.

In the world's childhood, near its radiant birth,
    In ages mystical and golden,
    When angel faces were beholden,
And godlike statues fell from heaven to earth,
    Had thy dread loveliness been found
    Haloing with light some spot of holy ground,
It had been worshiped as some Plastic Power
Which weaves the rainbow and the flower,
Or flames in purple at the morning hour.

From the cold rock the Hebrew Prophet brought
    The living waters sweetly glowing
    To fainting multitudes out-flowing ;
Such blessing art thou in the realm of Thought !
    No hapless futures with a dearth
    Of inspiration e'er shall scourge the earth,
While thou dost stand, a Fountain subtly riven,
Whereby fresh life may still be given,
And primal sympathies renewed with Heaven !

MY LYRE.

THE Lyre I touch with faltering hand
  Was never tuned in princely halls;
It was not framed in Music's land
  For fêtes and carnivals:
      A mystic birth
      On freer earth,
  Had it 'mid rocks and waterfalls.

I found it in the mountain wood,
  Hung high upon the forest tree:
The Winds that loved the solitude,
  The Waves that to the sea
      Bounded along,
      In light and song,
  Gave to these strings their melody.

And like the murmurs of the Deep,
  Still lingering in the spiral shell,
Unbidden, from their charméd sleep,
  Mysterious numbers swell,
    In grief or ire,
    Across my Lyre,
  Eolian wail or tocsin knell.

When brother-minstrels shall repair
  To glean my ashes from the pyre,
Like cloudlet melting into air,
  My loved and shadowy Lyre,
    Of fairy birth,
    Shall pass from earth,
  And join its own Primeval Choir.

THE POET AND THE BROOK.

POET.

SPARKLING child of nature ! why
Star-like glance so swiftly by ?
Every bird is hushed, unseen,
In his curtained tent of green ;
Every bee on open flower
Sheathes his wing this sunny hour ;
On the slope lies radiant June,
Sleeping in the lap of Noon ;
And the meadow now to thee
Would a nursing mother be ;
Cease thy childlike race, and rest
Softly on the meadow's breast !

BROOK.

Sweet the spot and bright the day!
But my waves must glide away
To adorn some other scene,
Brighten other banks with green,
Glimmer through the darkest woods,
Break the air of solitudes,
Bearing as they flow along
Joy and beauty, life and song.

POET.

Rocky chasm across thy way
Soon may weave thy shroud of spray,
Winter's breath from bleakest hill
Strike thee silent, cold and still.
Happier lie in ease and bliss,
Center of such group as this;
While at night the skyey train
From thy mirror shine again.
On such restless heart as thine
Stars of heaven can never shine!

BROOK.

Suns in distant, deep array,
Thou dost call the Milky Way,
All their glory lost to thee,
Glimmering through immensity :
So in every gleam I make,
As o'er chiming stones I break,
Sparkling fragment to thine eye,
Suns and systems pictured lie ;
For to him who labors most
Least of earth or heaven is lost,
And his form, however small,
Daguerreotypes the Sacred All.

POET.

Changeling ! ever dost thou roam,
Without country, without home ;
Nature vainly spreads her store,
Thankless thou dost yearn for more ;
Violets shed their sweet perfume
O'er their cradle and their tomb ;

And the birds enamored grow
Of some green, protecting bough :
All in motion, sound and spray,
What allures thy step away ?

BROOK.

Ah ! I hear the Ocean waves
Chanting in their coral caves,
With a melody that thrills
To their brethren on the hills,
Sweetly luring them along
To commingle in their song.
Passing from the summit gained
On to summits unattained,
Poet ! dost thou never hear
Voices from a brighter sphere,
Gently calling thee away
To the Heavens' eternal day ?

NOCTURNE.

Moonbeams, moonbeams everywhere!
On the water, in the air,
On the earth and at the door,
Round the walls and on the floor!
Hence! ye Spirits of the Night!
With your pale, sepulchral light.
Were the moon not glaring high
With her never-winking eye,
We could e'en believe ye were
Ghosts of sunbeams lingering here.
Blind am I with blaze of day,
To more willing eyes, away!

Kiss the shadows from their place
On the sleeping water's face;
When the subtle shadows fly
Make the waters seem the sky.

Pry into the sparrow's nest
At the brood around her breast;
O'er the misty meadow creep,
Charm the little flowers to sleep,
Make the purple, red and blue,
Glisten whitely in the dew,
Make the white ones still more white;
On the rifted oak alight;
Tip the church's spire afar
With the image of a star;
Glide into the garden bower,
Glimmer round the moldering tower;
Dip into the deepest shade
Whence the owlet's cry is made;
Hang a shroud on aspen tree
Rustling, swaying fitfully,
Or to sleeping churchyards hie
And on spectral marbles lie.

Endless watch have I to keep,
Her sweet eyes are hushed in sleep,
Folding like an Eastern rose
Her sweet soul has found repose;

Speak no more her silent eyes,
And the rose still folded lies!
On a love-wind swift I fly,
To the shadowy grotto hie:
There lost Florence I can see
As she ever seems to me.
Glowing and serene she stands,
Parted lips and folded hands,
Flood of sunlight on her hair
And her features marbled there!
Would those lips one word reply
E'en its echo could not die!
Could one smile those features give
E'en its shadow sure would live!
But she stands forever so,
In her weird, auroral glow,
Half of violet, half of snow;
Like some statue, brightest one
In a palace of the Sun!

What is Sleep but mental night?
Dreams its pale, sepulchral light,
Ghostly shadows of our Thought
Strangely on our being wrought;

Glimmering o'er our deep repose
With their false, ideal shows,
Some in beauty, some in pain,
All to be dissolved again,
To chaotic forms away
At the touch of mental day.

MUSIC.

Give me music all the day!
  Bring to greet th' advancing morn,
Brisk to Pleasure's roundelay,
  Trilling pipe or jocund horn;
Whispering wind among the trees,
  Carol of contented bird,
Children laughing as they please,
  Bleat of flock or bell of herd.

When the burnished noon appears,
  And the snowy cloudlets shine,
In the wood of thousand years,
  Let me by the brook recline,
Whilst the glad waves, on their march,
  Tinkle round the twisted root,
Whilst I fill the forest arch
  With the sound of liquid flute.

When the torch of daylight fades,
  And the twilight air is still,
Let me from the shadowy glades
  Hear the lonely whip-poor-will;
Whilst sweet Reverie sits remote
  Fixed upon her favorite star,
And young Love's persuasive note
  Trembles on the light guitar.

When the moon has climbed the hill,
  Ushering silver evening in,
Let Devotion's ready skill
  Tune the solemn violin;
Let the organ's gradual swell
  Heavenward pour its mighty note,
And the toll of steepled bell
  O'er the aerial tissue float.

Thus shall Music all the day
  Lap me in its sweet control,
And the winds of nature play
  Through th' Æolian harp of soul.

THE WILD RE-UNION.

In the ages which we call benighted,
  And the Teuton's weird and wondrous land,
In an upmost story, dimly lighted,
  At a long and narrow wooden stand,
      Darkly stained with blood,
      The Dissector stood,
  Held a purpled knife within his hand.

'Twas late, and all his comrades had departed,
  Left him at his table there alone ;
On the dreamy Student, heavy-hearted,
  Midnight stars in silent wonder shone ;
      From his eyes there came
      Flashes as of flame,
  Born of sorrows to the world unknown.

To the churchyard in the moonlit meadow
Earthly hopes and earthly joys were borne ;
Stolen to the land of dream and shadow
From his bleeding heart her heart was torn ;
She his love allowed,
But her kinsmen proud
Had repulsed his gentle suit with scorn.

Droop'd the Lady with her crushed devotion,
Nourished and concealed the fatal flame,
When her heart had ceased its sacred motion
Sister to the angels she became ;
He, oppressed with grief,
Sought a faint relief,
In his studies of the human frame.

Quietly the youth a corpse uncovered,
Which the sunken drapery revealed,
Awful thoughts around him seldom hovered
Near the dead : his heart had sorrow steeled ;
Starting with a thrill,
Stood he then as still
As a brook by winter winds congealed.

Lay before him there a beauteous Maiden
(High-born damsel), stolen from the tomb,
Dead, but Death had not her features laden
With his characters of fearful gloom:
On her roseate face
Lingered every trace
Of her girlhood's gentleness and bloom.

To her breast the hair hung down in tresses,
Curling like the tendrils of the vine;
Ripe her lips were for the sweet caresses,
Flush with love and red as if with wine;
Of the purest gold,
And ethereal mold,
Finger-rings threw out their fairy shine.

Were the body and the chamber haunted?
For the youth could not remove his gaze;
Like a marble shaft he stood, enchanted,
And his eyes had frenzy in their blaze;
The Dissector's room
Lost to him its gloom—
Was enveloped in a golden haze.

Hung with damask curtains seemed the windows,
O'er the mantel ticked the household chime,
Purple flames flared up from out the cinders,
Like a bed whereto a bride might climb
Seemed his table, high
And broad unto his eye,
Decked with sculpturings of the olden time.

Lovingly upon the snowy linen
Lay the form of Beauty he beheld ;
Mouth and eyes were sparkling, soft and winning;
In her breast the maiden fervor swelled ;
Manliest virtues melt,
He, enamored, felt
To her heart his throbbing heart impelled.

"Art thou, Lost One ! come from blissful Eden
To assuage my bosom's burning pain ?
Nevermore, O rare and radiant Maiden !
Shall the furies part our souls again !
Heaven will not divide
Bridegroom from his bride ;
Angels are singing now our marriage-strain !"

On her neck he fell, oppressed and panting;
  Blent his lips in madness with her own;
Round his form she locked her arms enchanting,
  Cold her arms as chiseled out of stone:
      Drooped his trembling head,
      Sight and hearing fled,
  And his soul dissolved in joys unknown.

When the sun threw from his burning quiver
  Ray-like arrows, beaming far and wide,
Stark and cold lay out the pallid lover,
  Silent at the lifeless maiden's side;
      Death was on his brow,
      Heaven had heard his vow,
  And he was not parted from his bride.

FAREWELL.

In vain, in vain have I essayed
  To speak the word "good bye:"
It lingers on my lips, sweet maid!
  And changes to a sigh.

And there's no need of Reason's wiles
  To break the pensive spell,
The heart that tells its joy in smiles
  May sigh its sad farewell.

We met when rival roses round
  In bridal beauty shone;
We part when on the Autumn ground
  The golden leaves are strown.

The rose was like Love's early power,
  So bright, so pure, so brief;
So sad, so drear our parting hour,
  'Tis like the falling leaf.

When on my lyre's enchanted string
  I try my tuneful art,
Two notes from out the chords shall spring
  And vibrate to my heart!

A note of joy that e'er we met
  Shall sweetly, briefly swell,
And leave a note of soft regret
  That e'er we bade farewell.

THE ORANGE FLOWER.

WITH sedulous care, in a Northern bower,
I nurtured a beautiful orange flower,
But it pined for scenes more sweet and fair,
And it died for love of its native air,
Like a Maid only lent to earth, not given,
And early wafted away to heaven.

And once I cherished a fruitless love,
For so it was written, they say, above;
A love as gentle, as pure, as bright,
As wonderful as the rays of light;
In happier hearts it might bloom and blow,
But it withered and died in my heart of snow.

LINES TO A YOUNG FRIEND.

In every material thing which we see
 Is something ethereal not to be seen;
There are Nymphs in the water and Sylphs in
  the tree,
 And summer-night Fairies that dance on the
  green.

The caskets thus sealed open not to our call,
 Nor give to our yearnings their mysteries up,
Yet spiritual essences live in them all,
 Like dew in the flower, like wine in the cup.

The rose as it blossoms, the star as it shines,
 The magic of music, the graces of youth,
Aurora and spring-times, are tokens and signs
 Of the presence of Angels of Beauty and Truth.

Whilst in the affections that gladden us here
  And lead us serenely to pleasures above,
In charity's sigh, and in pity's sweet tear,
  Are the best of the Angels, the Angels of Love.

O Thou! to whose Spirit these lines are addressed,
  Whom Nature has dowered with all that she
    could,
May thine outer adornment be inwardly blest,
  And the Beautiful prove but a shrine for the
    Good!

THE ROVING HEART.

My Heart was a rover
  And lived like the Bee,
Until it was Lover,
  Adored one ! to thee.

It sipped every blossom
  The gardens all o'er,
But ah ! from thy bosom
  It wanders no more.

Elate with its fleetness
  It spread the gay wing,
And gathered the sweetness
  From every bright thing.

But vain the endeavor
  To exhaust thee of thine,
So thou holdest forever
  This wild heart of mine.

LOVE ME ALONE.

THE mildew has blighted the blossom,
  Misfortunes have come like the tide,
And all the false friends of my bosom
  Have fled in distrust from my side ;
Sweet girl ! whom I love so sincerely,
  Come, bend your bright eyes on my own,
And with accents I treasure so dearly
  O say you will love me alone.

I vowed, and I thought they believed me,
  They vowed, and I swore to their truth ;
How many, alas ! have deceived me,
  And broken the pledges of youth !

But, Love ! your caresses can make me
  Forget every pang I have known,
And I care not what others forsake me
  If you will but love me alone.

Though Hope on the brink of perdition
  Stands palsied in silent affright,
Though the star of my early ambition
  May sink in the shadows of night ;
Life's Sun will continue to shine, Love !
  As bright as it ever has shone,
For you'll bend your sweet eyes upon mine, Love !
  And say that you love me alone.

LOVE'S THE ONLY TREASURE.

WITH many passions, great and small,
  We restless souls are living,
But Love's the sweetest of them all
  In getting or in giving:
For prior both in time and worth
  This sacred flame was given;
All others have been born on earth,
  But Love is part of heaven.
    Love me, love me, more and more,
      Love me without measure,
    Kiss me, kiss me, o'er and o'er,
      Love's the only treasure!

The star of Fame shines bright above,
  To many eyes resplendent,
But in our skies the star of Love
  Supremely is ascendant;

For Fame's false light will disappear
When you approach it nearer,
But penetrate to Love's sweet sphere
And it will shine the dearer!
Love me, love me, more and more,
Love me without measure,
Kiss me, kiss me, o'er and o'er,
Love's the only treasure!

Then as to Gold, much worshiped Gold!
Let sordid spirits prize it!
Since Love is neither bought nor sold
We freely can despise it.
For what is Gold to Love like this?
Correctly to appraise it,
A single smile, a single kiss,
Entirely outweighs it!
Love me, love me, more and more,
Love me without measure,
Kiss me, kiss me, o'er and o'er,
Love's the only treasure!

What envy, folly and distrust,
Surround the slaves of Fashion!

We would regard them with disgust
If 't were not for compassion.
Their love is but the love of power,
Of place, or jeweled splendor;
But true Love is a sacred flower,
As modest as 't is tender.
Love me, love me, more and more,
Love me without measure,
Kiss me, kiss me, o'er and o'er,
Love's the only treasure!

Whene'er you join in Pleasure's chase,
Remember that to-morrow
The rainbow smiles upon your face
May melt in tears of sorrow;
For every Pleasure has a sting,
And you are sure to find it,
Except sweet Love, the only thing
That leaves no pain behind it.
Love me, love me, more and more,
Love me without measure,
Kiss me, kiss me, o'er and o'er,
Love's the only treasure!

OLD AUNT HANNAH.

Let 's wait a little longer, Tom !
  Before we westward go ;
Let 's wait for old Aunt Hannah's sake,
  'T would break her heart, I know.
Look at her in her corner there,
  Her head is white as snow,
The last leaf of the good old tree—
  We can not leave her so !

In this old mansion was she born,
  Her joys and griefs were here :
How well she loved and nursed us all
  Through many a changing year !

See how she 's smiling at the fire
  And whispering something low !
She 's thinking of our Christmas times,
  O, long and long ago !

Beside yon crumbling garden wall,
  Our gallant father lies,
Our good, old mother at his side—
  Aunt Hannah closed their eyes !
She was the playmate of them both,
  Some fifty years ago—
To leave those dear old graves behind
  'T would break her heart, I know.

When the old soldier parceled out
  His treasures, great and small,
Aunt Hannah he would give to none,
  He gave her to us all.
We laid his good sword on his breast,
  For he had charged us so—
Whilst old Aunt Hannah knelt in tears—
  Ah ! Tom ! we can not go !

Her failing sands will soon be out,
  The kindly angel come,
And lead the good, old, faithful soul
  To our great Master's home.
And when we've marked her simple grave,
  And dropped a tear or so,
We'll urn the ashes of the past,
  And westward gaily go!

MY VALENTINE.

Now all the Birds in every grove
Devote their little lives to love,
But all their loves are naught to mine,
Since thou wilt be my Valentine!

With fairy speed the rosy Hours
Will bring the happy month of flowers,
On pleasure's bright, electric line,
Since thou art now my Valentine!

The summer trees in glen and glade
Will cast a soft, Elysian shade,
And with their fruitful arms entwine
Our evening bower, my Valentine!

When leaves autumnal fade and fall,
And pensive fancies come to all,
I, I alone will not repine,
For thou wilt be my Valentine!

Let Winter winds in fury blow,
Wrap all the world in shroud of snow,
Yet bright my mental sun shall shine,
For thou wilt be my Valentine!

When changeful Birds in other groves
Attune their vows to other loves,
Unchanging I will cling to mine,
For thou wilt be my Valentine!

KISSES.

"O Kiss me and go,"
  Said the maid of my heart,
And proffered her lip
  As a hint to depart—
"The midnight approaches,
  My Mother will know,
My kindest and dearest!
  O kiss me and go."

She gave me the blessing
  In such a sweet way,
The thrill of its pleasure
  Enticed me to stay.
So we kissed till the morning,
  Came in with its glow,
For she said every moment,
  "O kiss me and go!"

'T WAS LIKE A SILVER BUGLE.

He was a handsome stranger
  When first I heard him speak ;
But Love—it throbbed into my heart,
  And blushed into my cheek.
His words were few and simple,
  Nor were they meant for me :
But oh ! the tone—it was the soul
  Of love and melody !
    'T was like a silver bugle !
      The sweetest night in June,
    A silver bugle's serenade,
      Beneath the silver moon ;
    When lovers' evenings come so late,
      And morning comes—so soon !

When he confessed his passion,
  And all my maiden fears

Dissolved at once in perfect love,
Though only told in tears;
His words were blent with kisses
And few as they could be,
But oh! the tone—it was the soul
Of love and melody!
'T was like a silver bugle!
The sweetest night in June,
A silver bugle's serenade
Beneath the silver moon;
When lovers' evenings come so late,
And morning comes—so soon!

And now I am a mother,
With many cares beside,
I feel as happy and as young
As when I was a bride;
For when he takes at evening
The baby on his knee,
He speaks the words of tenderness
Which first he spoke to me;
O, like a silver bugle!
The sweetest night in June,

A silver bugle's serenade
  Beneath the silver moon ;
When lovers' evenings come so late,
  And morning comes—so soon !

LOVE IS OMNIPOTENT!

Summer-bright Beauty!
  Proud as thou art,
Love is omnipotent,
  Look to thy heart!

Lo! in the woodlands,
  Branches above
Bend to the warblers,
  Thrilling with Love.

And in the gardens
  Love is at play;
Butterflies twinkle
  Sportively gay.

Roses their sweetness
  Give to the bee ;
Lovers are kissing
  Under the tree.

Call not the breezes
  Spiritless things,
Sweet is the music
  Borne on their wings,

Gathered in countries
  Fairer than ours,
Given in whispers
  To the young flowers.

When the May-blossoms
  Sweeten the air ;
When the dew-diamonds
  Silver the hair ;

When the pure starlight
  Beckons above,
And the light lattice
  Opens to love :

Summer-bright Beauty
  Proud as thou art,
Love is omnipotent,
  Look to thy heart!

GOOD-NIGHT.

Good-night ! the clock has struck eleven,
Oh ! that to Time no tongue were given,
No sign to part my soul from thee ;
Good-night !—but wilt thou dream of me ?

Good-night ! the midnight hour has come,
And the last loiterer hastens home !
Go, take the rest I can not find,
Good-night !—but think'st thou Love is blind ?

Good-night ! the solemn stroke of one
Booms like a mournful minute gun ;
No tread disturbs the sleeping street,
Good-night—but stay, when shall we meet ?

Good-night! the bell is numbering two,
And hark! the cock too early crew;
Good night! but would it give thee pain
If morning never came again?

Good-night! alas! my Love! 't is three,
The envious dawn we soon shall see;
But night is coming to my heart,
Good-night!—but kiss me ere we part.

BEAUTIFUL! DIVINELY GLOWING!

Beautiful! divinely glowing,
  Heart! my Heart is thy true name;
For from thee a life-blood flowing
  Quickens and supports my frame.

When in pleasure or devotion
  Thy warm pulses faster move,
I, obedient to their motion,
  Throb with joy or blush with love.

When in grief or contemplation
  Thy sweet currents pause or fail,
Straight in mute ex-animation
  Sink I drooping, cold and pale.

Ah! if Time or Fate should sever
  Us who are no longer twain,
Heart, my Heart! no more forever
  Could I love or live again.

ORLEANNA.

THERE never was such beauty,
  Such radiant grace as thine,
There never, never was such love
  Nor such despair as mine.
The words to breathe my passion
  Have not been coined by man;
I do not tell thee what I would,
  But only what I can.

If tears could e'er have won thee,
  They had not ceased to flow;—
If blood—it had been freely spilt,
  O long and long ago!
I laid upon thine altar
  A gift beyond all price,
A true heart's worship—tears and blood
  Are no such sacrifice.

Of all life's blooming promise
  Of hope and peace bereft,
The only solace of my soul,
  My dreams (sweet dreams !) are left.
In dreams I plead my longings,
  And thou dost not reprove ;
In dreams I press thee to my heart
  And thou dost seem to love.

O would I were an old man
  With few more days to see,
And thou—my little darling child,
  To prattle on my knee.
My lot had then been happier
  Than this which now is cast,
And with thy radiance round my feet
  I had been blest at last.

O never from this parting
  We meet on earth again,
For I should give thee nought but love,
  Receiving nought but pain.

Nor let us meet in heaven
  Through ages yet to be!
Shouldst thou be still as beautiful,
  And still as cold to me.

Nay—nay—I could not love thee
  So well unless thou wert
The mate to my unmated soul,
  The twin heart of my heart.
Some hateful spell is on thee
  That here thou knowest me not;
But we shall meet and love in heaven
  When this is all forgot!

UNCLE JERRY.

Why, Jerry! what means all this sadness and fear?
  Here's your bitters, man! why do you cry?
Who told you I'd sell you? the trader that's here?
  By zounds, sir! he told you a lie!
When I sell the gold ring from my dead mother's
    hand,
  Or the sword which my grandfather bore,
When at Guilford his troopers made such a bold
    stand,
  I will sell you—and not before!

Why, don't you remember my face as a boy's,
  When often I sat on your knee,
Whilst you sang in your rugged, monotonous voice,
  Your foolish old ballads to me?

I wept at your sad ones and laughed at your gay,
  And made you repeat them all o'er;
Ah! when I forget my life's happiest day,
  I will sell you—and not before!

You made me the boat which I launched on the tide,
  And my traps for the birds in the snow;
You led my bay pony, and taught me to ride,
  And half the good things which I know.
You wept like a child when they sent me to school,
  To be absent for six months or more;
When you are a villain, or I am a fool,
  I will sell you—and not before!

If poverty's cup I am sentenced to drain,
  I will part with you—last of them all;
Your kindness, Old Jerry! would double my pain,
  And your sorrows embitter my fall.
If fate or misfortune should cause us to part,
  There's a God will unite us once more;
So drink my good health and console your old heart,
  And love me and serve, as before.

ISABELLE.

SLEEP, with rosy arm around thee,
Now hath bound thee,
Sleep thee well !
Thy dreams I will not waken,
Thou forlorn, forgot, forsaken
Isabelle !

O ! my heart is heavy laden,
Blighted maiden,
Isabelle !
For, though dead to love and duty,
Thy story and thy beauty
Have a spell.

All the flowers for thee have faded,
O degraded
Isabelle!
But th' eternal thorn is smarting,
And the pain it is imparting
Who can tell?

Ah! thy father under roses
Now reposes
Deep and well;
The grave dug by thine errors,
Was it watered with thy sorrows,
Isabelle?

See! thy little sister, playing,
Laughing, straying,
A gazelle
In the sunshine of the meadow,
Unvisited by thy shadow,
Isabelle!

But a dark eye is thy brother's—
And thy mother's,
Mark it well!

It is blind with watches keeping,
It is blind with weeping, weeping,
Isabelle !

It is too late to warn thee,
And to scorn thee,
Isabelle !
Is not for him who knew thee,
Ere that which makes him rue thee
Yet befell.

O sweet slumber ! touch her lightly,
Dreaming brightly,
"All is well ;"
Though the dark ones round her hover,
And no angels can recover
Isabelle.

O sweet slumber ! leave her never,
But for ever
Fix thy spell ;
Lie henceforth in sleep enchanted,
By consoling angels haunted,
Isabelle !

Never feel again the aching,
And heart-breaking
Of this hell ;
Nor to retribution waken,
Thou forlorn, forgot, forsaken,
Isabelle !

THE POET'S DIADEM.

O! WEAVE the Poet's diadem
  Of all the flowers with those,
His heart is strangely linked to them—
  The Cypress and the Rose.

So when some saddening hand of woe
  Shall touch his spirit-string,
The Cypress-leaf may darkly glow
  And shade the child of Spring.

And soon as smiling pleasure pours
  Her balm upon his grief,
The Rose may spread her breathing flowers
  And hide the Cypress-leaf.

THE DREAM OF THE ROSE.

THE moonbeams in a garden bower
Lie bright on every sleeping flower,
While Fancy's airy trains disclose
A vision to the fragrant Rose.

A radiant Maiden wanders by
The Charming One to many an eye;
The Rose's wish is unexprest,
But still she takes it to her breast.

It feeds on Beaüty's golden smile
Entranced in love, and thinks the while,
That nestled to her glowing heart,
No tint can fade, no bloom depart.

But see! the breeze too roughly blows,
Shakes the frail leaves and wakes the Rose;
Yet not alone, sweet Flower! repine,
My own false dreams resemble thine!

THOSE HAZEL EYES.

THOSE hazel eyes, those hazel eyes!
In vain my restless spirit tries
    To banish from my sight;
They gild my reveries with their beams,
They dance and sparkle in my dreams,
    They haunt me day and night.

Less radiant is the glance of morn
When night's dim veil is first withdrawn,
    No softer is the dove;
To witching smiles those eyes give birth,
And some are full of gentle mirth,
    And some of gentler love.

Sage Prudence spied the tempting snare
And whispered to my heart, "beware!"—
But I delayed my flight,
Until the rays like links combined,
And round my fettered heart entwined
A chain of rosy light.

Should I obey ambition's call,
And burst this strange, delicious thrall,
The world would call it wise;
But Love has dearer joys for me,
And more than all the world I see
In those sweet hazel eyes!

THE POET'S SONGS.

THE Poet sang one summer morn,
    A winding streamlet by,
A lay of love and fancy born,
And as the waters sparkled on,
    They made a sweet reply,
    They made a sweet reply.

The Poet sang at mid-day tide,
    Beneath the branches high,
And little birds on every side
To emulate his music vied,
    And made a sweet reply,
    And made a sweet reply.

The Poet sang at twilight hour
    Beneath the rosy sky;
The evening breeze o'er field and flower
Crept like an unseen fairy power,
    And made a sweet reply,
    And made a sweet reply.

The Poet sang with warmer tone
    Beneath young Laura's eye;
And when he clasped her radiant zone,
And wooed the girl to be his own,
    She made a sweet reply,
    She made a sweet reply.

THE STREAMLET'S WARNING.

O! HASTEN, pretty Streamlet!
  O! hasten to the Sea,
Nor dally in this meadow,
  Elysian though it be.

The summer months are coming,
  The sun will rise in wrath,
And pour his burning arrows
  Upon thy winding path.

The sands will yawn to take thee,
  Thy rocks will all be dry;
Thy waves no more will whisper
  To the flowerets blooming by.

Delay not in this meadow,
  Elysian though it be;

But hasten, pretty Streamlet!
  O hasten to the Sea!

I can not leave this meadow,
  Nor hasten to the Sea;
I can not leave this meadow
  With its April witchery.

For the sun is bright and gentle,
  His kiss is sweet and warm,
And he mirrors in my bosom,
  The glory of his form.

Upon my banks so mossy
  The Roses have their seat—
The Roses and the Lillies—
  And I sparkle at their feet.

I sing to them so softly
  They bend and smile to me;
O, I can not leave this meadow
  And hasten to the Sea;
I can never leave this meadow
  With its April witchery.

"WHEN LOVELY MARY."

WHEN lovely Mary gave her word
  To meet me by the walnut tree,
Unless the rain at midnight poured,
  Unless "Mamma" awake should be :

My heart with pleasure melted o'er,
  And every pleasing sense was moved,
I felt I never knew before
  How much I loved and was beloved.

When lovely Mary kept her word
  And met me by the walnut tree,
The clouds were gone, the moonlight poured
  Its favoring smile on her and me :

And when I kissed her o'er and o'er,
  And every bar from bliss removed,
I knew I never felt before
  How much I loved and was beloved.

IDOLINE.

The only Angel e'er allowed
To break the ever-during cloud
Which separates our earth from heaven,
(Alas ! that e'er such boon was given !)
Came as a Maiden, pure and bright,
A figure of embodied light,
With beauty matchless and serene,
Whom loving men called Idoline.

She seemed the life-blood of my heart,
And of my soul the central part,
For from her sphere the current flowed
To which my very life I owed :

Did her glad pulses faster move,
I warmed with joy or blushed with love ;
Did her sweet motions pause or fail,
Then sank I, drooping, cold and pale ;
She was the all-bestowing Sun,
And I a form she shined upon.

But ah ! what change has Fate decreed !
Just as I thought Hope's glorious seed
To flower and fruit would soon expand,
Death's Angel touched her with his wand.
To fields and palaces of light
Her Spirit took returning flight ;
The empty tenement of mind
For human tears was left behind,
More beautiful in deathly grace
Than all the animated race.
Where men her radiant form entombed
A golden willow sprang and bloomed,
In which a soft Æolian tone
Forever made melodious moan ;
And orient birds, ne'er seen before,
Came from some undiscovered shore,
And sang what men shall hear no more.

From angel tear-drops on the ground
A thousand flowers grew up around,
A thousand flowers to us unknown,
With shapes and colors of their own,
As if a rainbow fell from heaven,
Into a thousand fragments riven.
Perhaps their germs were wafted far
On ether's wave from evening star;
Perhaps there came, instead of worm,
A vital essence from her form,
Which wakened the compliant sod
To life and beauty born of God.

For days, for weeks, alone and mute,
With sense mysteriously acute,
I heard the sounds of other spheres,
Too far remote for human ears,
And saw by strange, magnetic light
Things unrevealed to human sight!
But all the myriad forms that fill
The theater of nature's skill,
In their interior splendor seen
Bore trace of the Seraph Idoline.

Time touched with his oblivious breath
The memory of her life and death,
And half my sorrows did allay
By taking half my joys away ;
But I would gladly feel the pain
To have the joy recalled again.

Sometimes I 've fancied that there came
Her accents calling on my name
From golden valleys glimmering far
Beneath sweet twilight's pendent star ;
Sometimes I 've felt, at morning hour,
Such wondrous, renovated power,
So calm and strong, so free and bright,
So girdled with prophetic light,
That I could vow my soul had been
In dreams with the Seraph Idoline.

FIDELÈ.

FIDELÈ! erring one! what claim
O Faithless! hast thou to that name?
Fidelè! faithful only to thy shame!

Poor alien from thy home and kin!
With that alluring smile of sin,
Which mocks, but can not hide the hell within:

Thou wanderest down the world forlorn,
Its guilty plaything and its scorn,
Thy soul a flower impaled upon a thorn.

When Eden lost thou dost recall,
Are cherub faces on its wall,
Or flaming swords that banish and appal?

Fidelè, see! through years of woe,
That little group—how bright they glow!
The old sweet home, the shaded portico,

Thy smiling mother, soft and fair,
Thy fairy self with golden hair,
And that pale boy, love-lost and statued there!

I wonder what thy thoughts may be!
Thy mother's thoughts are prayers for thee;
And mine are tears! What else is left to me?

DESERTED.

November's breath has chilled the morn,
And Winter's gathering scowl I see ;
The birds have fled the leafless thorn,
As my young joys have fled from me.

The flowers of Spring revive again,
When Winter's dreary night is o'er ;
But ah ! ye cheer my heart in vain !
The flowers of hope will bloom no more.

O mother ! mother ! fare thee well !
Forgive my perjured love for this ;
Lay on my heart an immortelle,
And seal mine eyelids with a kiss !

THE DESECRATED CHAPEL,

A SWEDISH LEGEND.

A CHAPEL by the Baltic shore
  Stood on a knoll of green,
Far out at sea, a league or more,
  Its gilded spire was seen.

But wicked Barons of the land
  Drove forth the saintly priest,
And met upon that quiet strand
  To keep unbridled feast.

They tore the pictures from the wall,
  They broke the sacred spire,
The altar and the benches all
  To feed th' unholy fire.

They rode the ring, the spear they sped,
  They broke the glittering lance,
They quaffed the wine and gaily led
  Their ladies to the dance.

But while they stunned the waning night
  With sound of boisterous glee,
A storm arose, with hoarded might,
  And burst upon the sea.

The sea forsook its ancient path,
  And rolled upon the shore,
It lashed the sloping hills in wrath,
  And inland sent its roar.

And when the waves sank to their place,
  Of chapel on the green,
Of lords or ladies, not a trace
  Was longer to be seen.

But still they say sometimes a light
  Gleams upward from the sea ;
The Baltic sailor hears at night,
  Mysterious melody.

He gazes down the placid deep
  Enchanted at his oar,
But lo! the sky's bespangled steep
  Is mirrored there no more.

The knoll is seen, the torches glance,
  The chapel reappears;
Fair ladies tricked for merry dance,
  And knights with golden spurs.

They kneel upon the emerald sward,
  And heavenward fix their eyes,
Whilst "misereres" to the Lord
  In solemn chant arise.

So weirdly from the buried shore
  Gleams up the fearful light,
The Baltic sailor bends his oar,
  And flies the phantom sight.

LOVE IN SEARCH OF TRUTH.

AN ALLEGORY.

When Love was sovereign Queen alone,
And had no partner to her throne,
She sought one day a great magician
Renowned for power and erudition,
Bearing a portrait in her hand,
And softly gave her high command:
"This is my Bridegroom, only he—
The child was lost in infancy,
Of birth divine, his name is Truth,
And I have come to seek the youth.
Adjust your mirrors, let me see
If one who bears the name is he."

The crystal flashes, and behold!
A stately figure, stern and old,
A man majestic, solemn, slow,
With lips compressed and eyes a-glow;
One hand upon a globe at play,
While books and papers round him lay:
'T was History's great self she saw,
And Love regarded him with awe;
But still her quick, discerning eye,
No semblance to the boy could spy;
She shook her head; his claim was banished,
And straight the great impostor vanished.

A second glance revealed to view
A face which more attractive grew;
A high-browed, melancholy man,
Across whose features, lean and wan,
Great thoughts like coruscations ran.
It was Philosophy, from toil and din
Abstracted to his world within.
Love gazed, and readily detected
Some features of the Child reflected,
But much too faintly to proclaim
That Truth and he could be the same.

Next sage Theology appeared,
From high devotions thus unsphered.
His face serene, his eye upturned,
A halo round his forehead burned,
One hand upon his heart was laid,
The other pointed o'er his head.
Love looked with joy—" It is his brother !
One outline is so like the other ;
But still, if narrowly you scan,
This child could never make such man ;
Here is too much of heavenly birth
To be so shadowed, e'en on earth !"

Again her notice is invited,
A glorious Youth she sees, delighted,
With pencil in his glowing hand,
Whilst radiant statues round him stand,
And music swells in soft vibrations :
'T is Art amid his own creations.
Love hastened gladly to compare
Pictures so beautiful and rare,
For twins they were at least by nature,
Identical save in one feature ;

Art's eye was blacker than the raven,
While Truth's was brightly blue as heaven.
The scenery passed dissolving by,
And Love dismissed it with a sigh.

"No more, Magician? What—no more?
Hast thou exhausted here thy lore?"
"None claiming to be Truth remains
But a poor Youth, not worth your pains;
An idle, vain, fantastic creature,
The freak and bunglework of Nature:
A harmless man of solitude,
Rambling in Spring-time through the wood,
In needless tears or silly gladness,
Rhyming and singing in his madness—"
"Show me his image," Love replied—
"If he be Truth—I am his Bride."

Once more the magic mirror turned,
'T was Poesy that Love discerned;
Seated serenely in a nook,
Studying a flower as 't were a book;
A spirit child-like and demure,
Bright as the diamond and as pure.

Love eyed the pictures—that and this,
And gave both this and that a kiss:
"Here is the bud and there the blossom,
The lord both of my throne and bosom!
Magician, haste! the tidings spread,
For Truth is found and Love will wed!"

ONE OF MARION'S MEN.

Good people of the Poor-house !
  Come round me at my call ;
By night or day, at work or play,
  I 've lived in peace with all ;
And now death lies upon mine eyes,—
  The owl hoots in the glen—
I 'll tell unbidden what long I 've hidden,
  I was one of Marion's men !

Yes ! yes ! the poor old pauper
  Once wore with youthful pride,
An epaulet (I keep it yet !)
  And a saber at his side.

I 've rode all night, in chase or flight,
  I 've rode all day—and then
In saddle away ! till another day,
  The best of Marion's men !

Away, in scour and scurry !
  O'er hills and swamps away !
For liquor and ladies, "the ever-readies,"
  And readier for the fray !
O ! you have heard how we did beard
  The lion in his den !
Or glide from sight like ghosts of night—
  Hurrah for Marion's men !

Ah ! many a gallant comrade
  Was laid where he did fall,
And some, in woods and solitudes,
  Were never buried at all—
But better far the fate of war,
  A glorious death ! and then—
No bread to crave, no pauper's grave
  For one of Marion's men !

I here confess my follies,
  I drank and played too fast!
'T was frolic living and reckless giving
  That brought me here at last.
But if this hour I had the power
  I 'd make a feast—and then
You 'd drink aright, a long good-night
  To one of Marion's men!

I went to prayers and preachings
  But few times in my life:
Ho! ho! the jokes on your Christian folks,
  Who live in trouble and strife!
God has control of my poor soul,
  He gave it and takes again—
Saint Peter's gate will open straight
  To one of Marion's men!

To all whom I have injured
  Would I could make amends!
The world with me did ne'er agree,
  But we will part good friends!

Let some one make, for pity's sake!
A head-board; chalk it then
In my behalf, with this epitaph,
"He was one of Marion's men!"

CIRCE FOR CALYPSO.

HE plied his shining oars
  Athwart the placid sea,
And scanned the swiftly passing shores
  To windward and to lee:
For pleasure's magic realm he sought,
  Calypso's happy isle;
In sweet Calypso's arms he thought
  To live and love awhile.

His bark flew o'er the sea,
  His soul flew o'er the air;
For whilst his oars dipped fast and free
  He dreamed that he was there.

O brightly rose the purple hills,
  O sweetly shone the vale,
O gaily chimed the rippling rills,
  O softly sighed the gale.

Serenely, faintly blew
  The silver bugle horn!
His soul the signal music knew
  And pressed in madness on.
Calypso's palace gleamed afar,
  Like sunset o'er the sea:
Long time he gazed entranced—but ah!
  Alas! O where was he?

The vision disappeared
  Like melting dream away;
In darkening waters deep ensphered
  An isle before him lay;
A vast and melancholy reach
  Of wild unbroken woods;
Uncheered by sound of human speech
  Its shadowy solitudes.

Fast fell the fearful night
  Upon his quaking heart ;
He saw the weird, phosphoric light
  Where Circe dwelt apart ;
Whilst growled and roared from cave and den
  The bears, the dogs, the swine,
The snakes, the wolves—which once were men,
  And drank of Circe's wine.

RELIGIOUS INSPIRATION FROM NATURE.

Wandering at ease one quiet Sabbath morn,
I cared not whither, in the forest shades,
List'ning the spirit-song which Nature sings,
I met a Maiden, rambling like myself,
Full of sweet morning fancies and hope-dreams.
When our glad eyes each caught the other's light,
Some pleasing instinct taught us that we were
Each for the other formed. I asked her not
Whether she were a Dryad of the wood,
New extricated from her leafy thrall,
Or a bright Naiad from some shining brook
Which fondly chid her for his lonely hours,
And wept her long delay. We found a seat

Fragrant and soft upon the cool green grass
That velveted the bosom of the wood.
Young birds with azure wings lit on the trees,
Whose new-leaved branches trembled over head,
And sang their loves. Across the welkin blue,
Flecked here and there with islands of bright cloud,
Shining Apollo drove his golden prow,
Attended by the swift and silent Hours.
We heeded not their flying—all entranced
In the kind interchange of genial thought ;
Nor could my will restrain the tender words
That live on poets' lips and long to pass
Low-whispered into Beauty's listening ear.

Ye Churchmen ! who delight in crowded aisles
And the loud chanting of the pompous choir,
Chide as ye choose ! More dear to me the sky
With silver-tinted clouds, the woodland-voice,
The many beautiful forms of forest-life,
The intercourse of happy human hearts,
And more accordant to the Sabbath-light,
And to the Spirit of Eternal Love
Which lives and thinks and moves in every thing,
Than all the dim religious shows of Art !

We parted not until the evening star
Displayed his glittering shaft, at which bright sign
The sweet Egeria of my yearning soul
Withdrew her hand from mine, and glided through,
Swift as an irrecoverable dream,
The forest's gathering shades. The rose she plucked
From out her bright brown hair and gave to me
Dissolved in air, and in its place the light
Of inextinguishable faith and love
Sank deep into my heart. The day's delight
Had lull'd my spirit to so sweet a calm,
That as the twilight cheered my homeward way,
I heard, or plausive fancy deemed she heard,
The Angel-choirs far chanting in the West
From sapphire palaces their Evening Hymn.

TRANSCENDENTALISM.

Heart! my Heart, why such a pining
  For some Chosen Thing to love?
Is not boundless Beauty shining
  On thee, round thee, and above?

Can'st thou not in saintly vision
  Blend thee with the Perfect Whole?
Lose thyself in joy Elysian
  With the Universal Soul?

Bow thee to Ideal Duty,
  Worship at no sensual shrine,
Corporate thyself with Beauty,
  So eternal, so divine.

Be a Feeler, not a Doer,
  Passive yield to Nature's tide,
Be to morning stars a wooer,
  Take sweet April for thy bride.

Never from such cold refining
  Living, lasting bliss can spring,
And my Heart, my Heart is pining,
  For some One, some Chosen Thing!

THE OLD MUSICIAN.

Haggard and pale the desolate old man
Lay in the sunshine of the market place
One beauteous day in summer.

That spot had been his only home for years,
And the sweet faces of the friendly stars
His only night companions.

People were gathering curiously around,
For a strange light spread o'er the beggar's face—
Death's solemn inspiration.

"Goldoni! Pupil of my better days,
Bring hither now the ancient violin
Wherewith you ravish Naples,

"For I believe the spirit of my youth
Is mantling o'er me with the warmth and light
And glory of the morning."

He passed the bow across the trembling string,
And after some premonitory tears
Began a plaintive measure.

The concentrated sorrows of his life
Floated upon the soft Italian air
In tender undulations.

He played—with eyes serenely turned to heaven,
Goldoni kneeling silent at his feet,
And the good people weeping.

He paused and smiled—the silver cord was loosed!
And the weird voices of his breaking heart
Died trembling into silence.

His face kept smiling whilst the angel-troop
Which took the beggar from the rich man's gate
Bore off his risen spirit.

Goldoni, weeping o'er the old's man's neck,
Heard from the opening doors of heaven afar
Such holy strains of music,

He never drew an earthly note again,
But consecrated his immortal powers
To spiritual devotion.

THE IDIOT NEGRO.

How darker than the pall of common night
Is man's estate when from his clouded soul
The inner sunlight fades away! How drear
And like a silent tomb is that dark mind
Which Reason leaves and yet which Madness spares!
I knew an idiot Negro in my youth,
A weak old man, half bent, and sad, and slow,
With crispéd hair as hoar as morning frost.
He had been happier in his early day;
Quick of perception, stout of heart and limb;
But changes came, and waning by degrees
The taper of the mind went out at length,
And left its chambers in Cimmerian gloom.
With trembling hand upon his knotted staff

So little seemed he like a living thing
That the dull ox removed not from his path
As he came toiling by. An humble look,
The stamp of long obedience, and a smile
Which had no meaning in its vacancy,
Made every feeling passer pause and sigh.
His master tasked him with no daily toil,
But to the woods and to the pleasant hills
He wandered forth, on no particular course,
But like a ship whose pilot leaves the helm,
Drifting away as any wind may choose.

Freedom, the sweet consoler, came too late;
He knew her not. Unnoticed circled round
The sights and sounds and motions manifold
Of this all-vital world. Upon gray stones,
And by decaying trunks of olden trees,
He leaned downcast like an insensate thing,
Or gathered to his hat, with scrupulous care
And muttered words, the leaves about his feet.
The ant was busy in her earthen cell;
The bee hummed by on his unwearied wing;
The nodding blue-jay twittered as she sought
The reeking earth-worm for her callow brood;

The speckled fish, pursuant of his prey,
Clove the bright waters with his silver fin;
The sleek-haired mole, toiling invisible,
Hoarded the acorns in his burrowed home;
All things, the meanest even, were instinct
With life and liberty, with hope and love,
Save him who sat alone, a broken link,
Fallen useless from the mighty chain of things.

Thus long he lived, for busied with the crowd
Of loftier objects for his tireless dart,
Death marked him not. And when the tyrant came
The victim shrank not from his chilling grasp,
But calm, as a blind man who stands unmoved
Upon the dreadful brink of an abyss,
Could not distinguish his stern enemy
From a familiar friend. 'T was but a step
From his dark state of being to the grave.

Few now can show his lowly resting place.
The wild grass overgrew th' unchiseled stone,
The briar unchecked has interlocked her thorns
Around the head-piece, and th' approaching tread

Might make the coward hare scud from her form
And fright the wood-thrush in her matted nest;
But there will come a time, a blessed time,
When the unaltered soul which here we saw
Like an enchanted statue, shall awake
As from a long, long sleep without a dream.

THE SOUTHERN MAN.

Is the festive banquet spread ?
  Shall merry Bacchus reign ?
Is it whisky pale or brandy red ;
  Is it claret or champagne ?
    Clink your glasses O,
    Tipple it while you can ;
But boys ! I 'm thinking, for social drinking,
  There 's none like the Southern man !

Is it a friend who needs
  The help of words or gold ?
Is it a sight of woe that pleads,
  Or a tale of sorrow told ?

Hearts and purses wide !
Scatter whate'er you can ;
But for generous living and cheerful giving,
There's none like the Southern man !

Is it the fiddle you hear ?
The ball-room in a glow ;
With the handsome lads and ladies dear,
Smiling all in a row ?
Call the figures loud !
Trip it light as you can ;
But for graceful dancing, till morn advancing,
There's none like the Southern man !

Is it a fight on hand ?
For sacred cause or none—
For a silly word or Fatherland ?
With a dozen foes or one ?
Clear the ring, my boys !
Battle it while you can ;
But for gallant bearing and reckless daring,
There's none like the Southern man !

Is it a lass to woo ?
Some idol to adore—
Amongst the black eyes or the blue,
The rich belles or the poor ?
Ladies ! mark my words,
And profit if e'er you can :
For ardent loving and faithful proving,
There 's none like the Southern man !

Is it the just and right ?
Is it the good and true ?
Aid it and bless it with all your might,
Whether it 's old or new.
Give it heart and hand !
Uphold it the best you can :
But for honest dealing and true, good feeling,
There 's none like the Southern man !

THE MINE.

I TREAD a dark and cheerless mine,
  Unnumbered feet below,
Where April mornings never shine,
  And violets never grow.

But far above, as fancy deems,
  Commingled sounds I hear,
Music of birds, and winds, and streams,
  Falls faintly on my ear.

Such is our home, this dreary earth
  To our dark natures given,
But sounds of an immortal birth
  Come to our souls from heaven.

SUNSHINE.

THERE lies the sunshine on my floor,
  So soft, so pure, so bright!
A message from the Spring out-door,
  A fragment of its light,
To woo me from my dreary mood,
And call me forth to field and wood.

Shine on, sweet Light! I can not steal
  To forests, streams and bowers
As in my boyhood, for I feel
  The load of painful hours;
But I accept thy golden cheer,
And smile amid my sorrows here.

'T is thus into our hearts from heaven
  Comes down the ideal ray,
By guardian spirits kindly given,
  A love-beam on our way,
A solace for our mortal cares,
Prophetic of celestial spheres.

"ALL IS WELL."

When Aurora's hands have spun
Golden vestures for the sun,
From the radiant eastern hill
Voices on the ether thrill,
Like the Morning Angels crying,
To the Guards of Night replying
"All is well,"
And in earthly echoes dying,
"All is well."

In the dusty, burning clime,
Toiling in the noon of Time,
Lo! the fainting reaper hears
Music from serener spheres,

Like the ripples of a river,
Whispering, surging, ceasing never,
"All is well,"
Surging, whispering on forever,
"All is well."

When the broken hues of light
Fade upon the western height,
Sacred hymnings from afar
Float from evening's gentle star,
Like the Guardian Souls who lead us,
Calling from the heavenly meadows,
"All is well,"
Calling to this world of shadows,
"All is well."

THE OLD COUNTRY CHURCH.

It was a spot to calm the fretted mind,
To wean the heart from transitory things
And turn to heaven. Upon a hill remote,
Embosomed in a brotherhood of trees,
The ruined Church appeared. The wooden stile
Had rotted to its fall, the leaning fence
Creaked in the wind of summer. Grass had grown
Across the path and ventured to the door.
Luxuriant boughs lay on the swagging roof,
Which, like the face of some old rock, appeared
Rugged and brown and covered o'er with moss,
Dripping with moisture. Through the shattered panes
The swallow passed with straw upon her bill,

Or earth-worm for her young. The prowling poor,
Or passing emigrants hard by encamped,
Had broken the shutters for their evening fire.
The humbler graves, that once were decked with
flowers,
The head-boards gone, the footstones all displaced,
Were sunken deep and full of withered leaves.
The slender railing which had once inclosed
The separate family had fallen down
And let the intruder in. Rankly the weeds
O'ertopped the battered monuments, and hid
The rural records of forgotten things.

Such was the spot: and there in autumn time,
When parting sunshine clad the distant hills
In all the golden drapery of eve,
Have I reclined for hours, and unappalled
By the unmoving specters of the place,
Silence and Desolation, have called up,
By sweet imagination's fairy power,
The long entranced Spirit of the past
For my companion. Warming Memory
Relit the pleasing pictures that for years

Were latent on the canvas of the soul.
The vestiges of rank decay were gone,
And the bright Sabbath brought the eager crowd
To the old Church again. The rustic vehicles
Groaned o'er the stony road. Along the fence
And by the trees the patient horses stood.
The plain old elder of the flock was there,
Close to the desk, and lined the ancient psalm ;
The portly matron in her snowy cap,
Slyly observant of the pranking boy ;
The bare-armed infant on the nurse's knee ;
The buxom girls, unconscious of their charms,
Or archly imitative of the town ;
The awkward stripling, whose untutored face
Betrayed his artless love ; the minister
With kindly look and gentle word for all,
Austere and chilling only in his creed.
I heard the prayer, and the concluding hymn,
Whose echoes lingered round the jutting eves
And dipt away into the quiet wood.
But with the glimmering of the twilight hour
The spell would break, and the approaching
shades
Unpeople the old Church again.

But still,
Though human footstep rarely treads the scene,
Nature hath left her sounds and colors there,
And many beautiful forms of forest life
Surround the spot and evermore maintain
Inaudible worship of the Deity.
The birds fulfill their offices of love
In every nook. The plaining stock-dove coos
All the bright noon-day from the rustling oak.
The truant bee and velvet butterfly
Flit o'er the rugged mounds. From bench to bench
The cautious spider weaves his filmy snare.
The enameled serpent by the crumbling step
Enjoys the sunny beam. In the still night
The dreary owl and lonely whip-poor-will
Mourn to each other on the shuddering air.
The dews come softly to the hoary walls,
And moonlight sleeps upon the silent floor.

THE MYSTIC UNION.

A LIGHT of glory to our feet benighted!
  A voice of resurrection to the dead!
"E'en as the Father to the Son united,
  So shall ye be to Christ your living head."

What doth it mean? In these poor hearts of ours
  Can the Omniscient a sojourner be,
As sunbeams nestle in the souls of flowers,
  Or angels come to sleeping infancy?

Ah, yes! Rejoice, ye contrite broken-hearted!
  His Holy Presence dissipates your sin;
Remember how the raging storm departed
  From the lone ship when Jesus stept therein.

Oh ! let his Love, a sacred fire out-going,
  Consume each molten image from our sight ;
And be our spirits, to his Truth in-flowing,
  Transparent as the diamond is to light !

It is the soul which makes its own external ;
  All things are outbirths from her inmost sphere ;
Sunshines of peace on landscapes ever vernal,
  And wastes of winter come alike from her.

The love of God, the fealty which we owe Him,
  Grafted upon our hearts and fruitful there,
Will make the outward life a noble poem,
  By making first the inner life a prayer.

Is not the Holy, beautiful Ideal
  The Father of our hope and joy and love ?
Which comes incarnate in the grosser Real,
  Remolding it by patterns from above ?

Joy springs from sorrow, virtue from temptation,
  And daily death is but a happier birth ;
Then comes our Sabbath of regeneration,
  Uniting heaven for evermore with earth.

THE STREAM OF LIFE.

As gayly down the stream of Time
  Fast glides this bark of ours,
The heart should swell to pleasure's chime,
  The bark be trimmed with flowers.

Ethereal music fills the sail,
  And rainbows span the prow,
Prophetic sounds of evil fail,
  And angels guide us now.

They say this wave, whose whispering gush
  Is soft as slumber's breath,
O'er darkling steeps and rocks will rush
  Into th' abyss of death.

Believe it not! At close of day,
  Whilst dreaming safe we lie,
This stream will bend its upward way
  Towards the evening sky;

Will glide through clouds of pearl and gold,
  And plains of azure too,
In light and music softly rolled
  To heaven's eternal blue.

So gayly down the stream of time
  Fast glides this bark of ours,
Our bosoms swell to pleasure's chime,
  Our bark is trimmed with flowers.

THE INFANT IN HEAVEN.

WHERE Death, in yon deserted ground,
His garnered harvest keeps,
Beside a small and verdant mound,
A lonely Mother weeps.

Upon the glittering turf she sits,
Like one in mournful dreams,
The trusting bird around her flits,
So motionless she seems,

In attitude of one whose mind
Implores a word of cheer,
Who e'en unto the whispering wind
Inclines an anxious ear.

She sees by more than fancy's light
  The pale, cold face below,
Whose infant roses were so bright
  A few sad days ago.

Meanwhile, beyond the curtaining skies,
  The Lost One finds his rest,
And leans, with love-illumined eyes,
  Upon an angel's breast.

Whilst angel-sisters deck his brow
  With their immortal flowers,
And lulling music whispers low
  Through the celestial bowers.

A nursling of the heavens, he lives
  In heaven's eternal bloom ;
But Nature's holy tie survives
  The passage of the tomb :

For list ! what does the loving breeze
  Unto the mourner speak ?
And see ! a sunbeam through the trees
  Hath kissed the mourner's cheek !

O, weeping Mother! couldst thou read
  The symbols round thee given,
Thy gladdened heart would surely heed
  These messages from heaven!

CONSOLATION FROM NATURE.

O! SEEK a pleasant valley
  When thy soul is full of care,
Or a forest, where the lulling wave
  Can ripple in thine ear;

Where the winds are softly sighing
  Through the dark and solemn pines,
And the light upon the verdant ground
  In broken splendor shines;

Where the little birds unfettered
  Warble blithely as they please,
And the squirrel leapeth lightsomely
  Among his native trees.

The freshness and the silence
  And the beauty will impart
A balm unto thy fretted thought,
  A peace unto thy heart.

The lofty mountain waters
  Are shattered to and fro,
And find no peace until they glide
  Into the vale below;

In lowliness of spirit
  Our hearts are newly blest,
And thousand gentle stars of heaven
  Are pictured in the breast.

Nor is it all a fancy
  That the Spirits of the wood,
And those that haunt the meadow walks,
  Are Messengers of Good,

That hover kindly round us
  In every beauteous thing,
To sweetly steal our cares away
  And heavenly comfort bring.

THE PHILANTHROPIST AND THE CHILD.

PHILANTHROPIST.

THIS Canary must be free;
Nature's law is liberty!
Don't you know it is a sin
To keep this little bird within?

CHILD.

My sweet mother gave it me.

PHILANTHROPIST.

Oh the wicked tyrant she!

CHILD.

Some one else imprisoned it.

PHILANTHROPIST.

Mends the matter not a bit.
You must answer for its pain,
Give it liberty again.

CHILD.

I love the helpless creature so!

PHILANTHROPIST.

'T is a selfish love, we know.

CHILD.

It sings so sweetly every morn.

PHILANTHROPIST.

Sing yourself when it has gone.

CHILD.

'T was not born or nurtured here;
In this foreign clime, I fear,
Freedom would not do it good;
'T will freeze or perish in the wood.

PHILANTHROPIST.

Nature amply will provide,
All its wants will be supplied;

'T will "develop," when it 's freed;
Give the sacred Gospel heed.
Hear it—"Let the oppressed go free!"
Give this bird his liberty.

CHILD.

Ah! but if he flies away,
Will not ugly birds of prey,
Stronger, fiercer, pounce on him,
Tearing madly limb from limb?

PHILANTHROPIST.

He must take his equal chances,
Whilst "Progression" still advances.
"Higher Law" 's the one to bind most,
Let the Devil take the hindmost.

CHILD.

Though but a child, it seems to me
Such "higher law" is cruelty.
I'll not obey!

PHILANTHROPIST.

I 'll break the cage!

CHILD.

You 'll kill the bird!

PHILANTHROPIST.

I do n't engage
For what the consequence may be,
But "higher law" cries "liberty!"

CHILD.

You are unwise!

PHILANTHROPIST.

I 'll break the cage!

CHILD.

A Christian man in such a rage!
Now I believe, though weak and small,
You are no Christian man at all!

DESCENSUS AVERNI.

A MYSTICISM.

A Youth in the land of Immortals,
  Engirdled with love like a zone,
In the sunshine and glory of morning,
  Went dreamily wandering alone.

Far down to the borders of Aidenn,
  Far down to the crystalline walls,
O'er which to the spaces beneath them
  God's Light, like a cataract, falls.

In-drawn, he was fixedly pondering,
  With an ardor akin to strife,
On the questions which have no answers,
  And the awful riddle of Life.

With a feeling of dread to have wandered
  From the center of Heaven so far,
That the sun of its holy meridian
  Had dwindled almost to a star,

He gazed on the verdurous tissues
  That glittered and grew at his feet,
When he saw a most wonderful Serpent
  Glide out of its hidden retreat :

A rainbow of serpentine colors,
  Gold, silver, and crimson and green,
So like to the beautiful herbage,
  That its motions were scarcely seen.

It glided away like a Spirit,
  Like a thought which we can not retain,
And the Youth, of its splendor enamored,
  Sought after it over the plain.

He lost it mid grasses and blossoms
  That swayed in the sighing breeze—
And he came to a granite Fountain,
  In the shadow of odorous trees :

A Fount with a sculptured basin
  Of Paradise-water there,
As placid as if it was frozen,
  As lucid as if it was air.

Forgetting the ethereal nectars
  To innermost angels given,
He scooped in his shell-tinct fingers
  The marginal water of Heaven,

When a Dove with fluttering pinions
  Alit on his outstretched arm,
With the plaintive wail of a mother
  Who would shield her child from harm.

In the reckless thought of the moment,
  He brushed the sweet bird away,
The bird which had seen how the Serpent
  Encoiled in the water lay!

What a change in the world within him!
  And thence in the world without!
The old path he could find no longer
  However he turned about.

He saw naught but an iron portal
  That led to a desolate moor,
A region of stone-heaps and shadows—
  And he passed through the iron door.

THE MAGIC GARDEN.

I WALKED in the magic garden
That lies in the summer air,
Upborne by the purple mountains,
And cloud-encircled there :

A place of wonder and glory,
Where Nature has no control,
But outward things are the symbols
Of things within the soul.

Thus, Zephyr, the lonely shepherd
That piped in the orange grove,
Was the sound of my heart a-sighing
For some chosen one to love ;

And the rivulet's face of silver,
  As it looked to the azure heaven,
Was the light of my soul rejoicing,
  In the Truth which God had given.

On a path that sweetly meandered,
  Like a careless train of thought,
I revolved the sacred enigma,
  And found the answer I sought.

An Angel appeared before me,
  Or a Demon in bright disguise,
With a heaven of womanly graces
  Enshrined in her love-lit eyes.

With a face of superlative beauty,
  With features so strangely bright,
They shone in that radiant garden
  As a meteor shines in the night.

She stood in a golden halo,
  In a sphere of magical art,
An aura of musical motions
  That thrilled to my inmost heart.

She proffered a golden goblet,
  Brimful of a rosy wine ;
Her lips had just deepened its color,
  And she proffered it then to mine.

"O, this is the dew of Heaven,"
  She said, with a luring smile,
And my heart—O, it wildly fluttered
  With passionate throbs the while.

There had stood a rose-bush near me,
  With listening roses thereon—
But lo ! in a luminous moment
  The roses and leaves were gone :

And a rare and beautiful Maiden
  Came suddenly shining there ;
Like a soul from the dead arising
  She rose on the fragrant air.

She proffered a silver goblet
  Brimful of a crystal dew,
In the grasp of her pearl-tinct fingers
  It brighter and brighter grew.

"I give thee the water of Heaven,"
  She said, with a smile of light—
And my heart—O, it sweetly fluttered
  With the joy of a marriage night.

I gazed from one to the other
  In silent and deep debate,
The look of the one was Pity,
  The look of the other was Hate.

When lo! I beheld in the Maiden
  An expression of purest love,
Like the face of my angel-mother,
  Which I knew was shining above.

I drank of her mystical goblet,
  And by its revealing art
I saw that a venomous serpent
  Was gnawing the Syren's heart.

She paled like a cloud disappearing,
  And where she had stood there upgrew
The dark green leaves of the nightshade,
  And its berries of ghastly blue.

Then a star glanced up into heaven,
  And the garden dissolved into air,
Whilst I knelt at my eastern window,
  With my soul dissolved in prayer.

SPIRITUAL VISION.

Oh ! turn into my palace
  From thy weary, dusty way ;
A cup of wine shall glad thy heart
  And music cheer thy stay.

The crystal gate is open
  On golden hinge ajar,
And down the odorous avenues
  The portals gleam afar.

The myrtles and magnolias
  Give out Æolian tones,
And statues twinkle through the trees
  Enwrought of precious stones.

The mystic soul of Beauty
  Shall meet thee face to face,
For Peace the Angel fixes here
  Her charméd dwelling-place.

"What braggart words of folly
  Are these thou speakst to me?
Thou poor old doting mendicant,
  As blind as thou canst be!

"Thy wine is naught but watei
  Dipped from the rustic spring!
Thou hast no music here, unless
  The birds may choose to sing.

"I see a lowly cottage,
  Instead of kingly hall,
Thy avenues and sculptured gems—
  I see them not at all.

"Thy mystic soul of Beauty
  Is a phantom of thy brain,
Thy Angels must be Discontent,
  And Poverty, and Pain."

Now by thy thought outspoken,
  Poor wanderer ! I discern
How much of Love thou hast to feel,
  Of Wisdom hast to learn !

Go out into the highways,
  And speak the words of cheer ;
Return the joyful smile for smile
  The mourning—tear for tear.

Find thy own life in others,
  And then come back to me ;
And thou shalt hear what I have heard,
  And see what I can see.

The inner world of splendor
  Is sealed to carnal eyes ;
Invisible to selfish man
  Is saintly Paradise ;

But like the laughing Dryad
  Within the blooming tree,
There is a World within the World
  The Good alone can see.

THE SHEPHERD OF CYPRUS.

I HUMBLY thank you, Greek Philosophers!
Who come so far to hear a Christian talk,
Old, blind and wretched, to the beasts condemned.
I heard just now the hungry lion's growl,
And my flesh trembled, and my hair uprose,
But my true self was calm and unappalled;
Glory to Father, Son, and Holy Ghost!

No doubt you are weary of my simple words,
For preaching Christ is plain and spiritual,
Unlike your philosophic diatribes;
So I will tell you of a wondrous thing
Which happened when I was a shepherd boy
In my native Isle of Cyprus; whence began
My long discipleship to good St. John,
And my eternal bondage to the Cross.

One bright Spring morning, when the tender grass
Had just been moistened with a little shower
Like a child's tears, which a soft-coming wind
Sweet as a mother's lips, had kissed away,
My blue-eyed sister and myself led out
Our little flock, just twenty-four in all,
To feed them at the green, secluded foot
Of a lofty mountain. There we played awhile
Along the margin of a winding stream
Which skirted leisurely the mountain's base,
A silver hem upon its flowing robe
Of forest green, trying in vain to float
Young flowers new gathered from their juicy stems,
Like mimic gallies on the bright-faced water.
In careless sport at last we ventured in,
Planting our naked feet on golden sand,
And wading softly till the water-nymph
Clasped us, with cooling kisses, round the knees,
Making us laugh.

We gained the other bank,
Where we had never been before, when suddenly
We heard such wondrous music up the height,
That we forgot our flock and the dread chance

Of meeting some wild creature in the woods,
And followed it. We climbed the shaded slopes
So eagerly, we did not turn to see
The radiant picture which was spread below;
The town-built valleys, and the rock-bridged streams,
Green-growing pastures, and the purpled hills
O'erhung with shifting canopies of cloud;
And, too remote to hear its ceaseless sound,
The flossy white surf of the emerald sea,
Far shining up and down the golden-beach.

We climbed the wooded slopes, and as we went
We both began to glow, not with fatigue
But love, and when we paused, 't was not to rest
But to embrace each other, heart to heart,
To beg forgiveness and to be forgiven
For past offenses, and with tears renew
Our pledges of affection, strangely moved
By powers invisible. Thus on we went,
Upward and onward, hand in hand conjoined,
In atmosphere serene of peace and joy.

As we approached the summit, wondering much
How sweet and cool the sea-air was so high,

And peering vainly under every copse
For the strange sounds which had attracted us,
But which now ceased, we saw the Holy Man
Forth issuing from a dark and mossy grotto,
Whose entrance was o'erhung by netted vines.
He held a parchment in his hand ; his eyes
Were lambent with the light of heavenly love—
Light left upon him by the "open heaven"
Of which you read in his Apocalypse.
His locks were white as snow and soft as silk,
But still you never could have thought him old,
For a strange youthfulness shone in his face ;
His delicate features, like a rosy girl's,
Beaming with beautiful simplicity.

Outstretching to us both his long white hands
With an ethereal tenderness, he said,
"Children ! what brings you to my lone retreat ?"
"The music," I replied, abashed and low,
While my coy sister earnestly looked down,
Digging the soft turf with her little foot.
"Music ? I heard none"—was his slow response ;
But in a moment, with a sudden gleam
Of comprehension on his brow, he added,

"Ah! I perceive that you are blest of Heaven,
And are partakers of the spiritual sight.
You need no revelation more but this,
Love one another, for our Life is Love.
For thee, O bright and blue-eyed daughter of the vale,
Celestial angels keep impatient watch;
But we, young Shepherd! we shall meet again.
Behold the messengers which will conduct
Your wandering footsteps to their wonted paths!"
Smiling, he turned into the shadowy grot,
Casting a silver light upon its wall.

Then first we saw the Heaven-sent messengers,
As stars come out when sunlight disappears.
A milk-white Lamb, fair as another child,
Up started from my sister's feet and frisked,
Playfully gamboling as it moved in light
Adown the slope. With childish ecstasy
Clapping her hands, she started in pursuit
Of the bright creature. At my side I saw
A fiery Eagle with imperial eye,
Slowly unfolding his majestic wings
All silver tipped. He then appeared to move

In unison with something in myself;
Gliding serenely on from bough to bough,
Flitting and perching where mine eye directed,
As if he were the shadow of my soul,
Or echo of my thought.
Thus down we went,
And as we went I saw a lion couched
Upon the leaves asleep, his huge fore feet
Half-hidden by his brindled mane. We passed
Breathless on tip-toe by, and then descried
A great brown serpent dangling from a tree,
Like a vast spiral grape-vine, coil on coil,
Harmless, for some enchanter had been there
Lulling his fierce malignant soul to sleep.

Thus wondering, hurrying down we went, in all
The silence and the mystery of a dream,
Until we touched the bright-faced wave again;
When lo! the Lamb and Eagle disappeared,
Bright symbols, vanishing away like thoughts.
We crossed in trepidation, and looked back,
But every trace of mystery was gone;
We were surrounded by the common things
Which we had seen a thousand times before;

The old, familiar wind was in the pines,
And sunset slowly reddened up the steep.

I know you would now ask me if I take
These strange events for fact or metaphor.
Both—I reply; for Nature's outward forms
Are plastic to the molding breath of Spirit,
And every thing created in its turn
Contains a spiritual essence, which is truth.
Thus metaphor is spiritual wisdom couched
In natural language, and a miracle
Is but the outplay of a spiritual law
Into th' expanse of nature.

Would you know
More of these mysteries, for my time is short
And my strength failing, the great Comforter,
Who is the Spirit of Truth, will guide your spirits
Into all truth. My last hour I would spend
In solitary prayer. Remember what I told you
About the Resurrection. Good friends! adieu!

TRIBUTE

TO EMANUEL SWEDENBORG.

Lost from her altars, Nature's noblest Priest!
  On earth ignored, traduced, misunderstood,
Thou hast ascended to the empyreal feast
  With thy co-laborers, the Wise and Good.
Men, all too weak or blind the Truth to see,
  Would shroud thy grave in thickest pall of night,
Where Angels with prophetic smiles of light
    Have planted flowers of immortality.
Like mountain-peak emerging from a flood,
  In clouds and darkness lone thou standest now,
As to the ark one sacred summit stood,
  When all the world was sunk in waves below:

But in the future when the watery waste,
By the great ocean of God's Light displaced,
Shall of its ravage leave no mark to tell,
  Men in their vales shall view thee from afar
  Towering serenely by the Morning Star,
In height of glory inaccessible.

A HOME PICTURE.

THEY have wheeled the Old Man's easy chair
Under the blossoming cherry tree ;
For he still delights to hear and see
What Spring is about in the open air ;
For his heart is young, though his head is old,
And the light about him is purple and gold.
A bright-eyed Boy is at his knee,
And the Old man's trembling hands are laid
Crown-like, on his curly head.
A Picture beautiful to see !
How Age and Infancy agree
In loving, prattling sympathy !
While down the snow-white blossoms fall
Brightly, softly as they can,
Like blessings dropped by the Father of All
On the Winter and Spring of Man.

THE HERO'S GRAVE.

O LIGHTLY, tread lightly, 't is holy ground
Where the corse of the Hero is resting:
There's a charm on the mind and a spell on the mound,
Like a halo of glory investing.

For the Spirit that kindled the eye of the brave
Lingers still at the spot to endear it;
And his is the heart of a coward or slave
That beats not more gallantly near it.

Ah! shed not your tears at the soldier's lot,
When he dies where his country calls him,
When he falls ere the fire of the foeman's shot
Or the terror of death appalls him.

The smoke of the battle may melt away,
  And the turf of the valley may hide him,
His form in its braided shroud may decay,
  And his good saber rust beside him ;

But a light comes forth from the warrior's grave
  Whilst his comrades are sorrowing o'er it,
A beacon of hope to the hearts of the brave,
  And oppressors may tremble before it.

Then lightly, tread lightly, 'tis holy ground
  Where the corse of the hero is resting,
For the Spirit of Liberty hallows the mound,
  With a halo of glory investing !

DEATH OF GENERAL LEE.

"In the delirium caused by the fever, the last words that General Lee was heard to say were, 'Stand by me, my brave Grenadiers.'"—*Life of General Charles Lee, by Jared Sparks,* page 200.

No, no, I am not dying!
I need no priestly cares;
Away, away!
I will not stay!
I 'll join my grenadiers!

Hark to the booming cannon!
'T is music in my ears;
See! from this mound,
That battle-ground—
And these—my grenadiers.

Yon bristling, shining column !—
  What martial fire it stirs !
    By dint and brunt
    We 'll break its front ;
  Ready ! my grenadiers !

Charge on them now like meteors
  Shot swiftly from their spheres !
    Hurrah ! 't is done,
    The point is won ;
  Hurrah ! my grenadiers !

Those right-hand guns are silent !
  The wind of fortune veers ;
    Beat, beat the drums !
    A rescue comes !
  Lee with his grenadiers !

Down with the British bullies !
  Down with the Hessian curs !
    Follow me, all !
    I 'm shot ! I fall—
  On ! on ! my grenadiers !

Right on through smoke and carnage!
  Nor let him flinch who hears
    The crush of bones,
    Like clashing stones;
  Right on! my grenadiers!

Have ye not won the battle?
  Then give your deafening cheers!
    And should I die,
    Stand cheering by,
  My gallant grenadiers!

What means this wail of women?
  What mean these sobs and tears?
    How cold it blows!
    How dark it grows!
  Stand by me, grenadiers!

BEFORE AND AFTER THE BATTLE.

Is it the frost that glitters so white?
  Is it the wind in yonder glen?
No! no! they are tents in the early light,
  And that is the marshaling sound of men.
Bright over armies the morning shines,
  Shining as o'er a ruffled lake;
Dark lie the cannon along the lines,
  Like hurricane clouds before they break.
Over the hill and over the valley,
Wildly the buglemen call to the rally!
Float—banners! float—bright as the sunset;
Blow, bugles! blow—blow for the onset!

Is it a ruin, old and gray,
  That glimmers in dusky twilight so?

A ruin whose walls and people lay
  Mingled together in dust below—
O'er which a moon of lurid red
  Wanders, in smoky vapor lost—
No! no! 'tis the shadowy field of the dead,
  And the wreck of a broken host.
Over the hill and over the valley,
Ne'er shall the buglemen call to the rally!
Droop, banners! droop—droop like the willow;
Weep, Angels! weep o'er the soldier's pillow!

HOPE IN WINTER.

As those who, wintering in the Arctic seas,
Look round them vainly for the cheering sun,
Gone but not lost behind their Southern hills,
And in the gleaming snows, Auroral lights
And coruscations of the cloudless sky,
Discern memorials of the living fire
Of Heaven—and prophecies of its return :
So we, in thankfulness and patient hope,
Standing mid Winter's melancholy waste,
The unurned ashes of the year, have glimpse
Of blessings, beauties, glories which have been
And are again to be.

How dark and cold,
How desolate and foreboding are the forms

Which Winter's touch impresses on the world !
The stately trees, a troop of skeletons,
Tower in the gloom and wave their naked arms
Complainingly to the sky. With tinkling sound,
The ghostly echo of its summer laugh,
The brook goes stealing through its frosted banks,
Or, chilled by north-wind kisses to repose,
Lies white and silent as a water-nymph
Outstretched, and in the moonlight fallen asleep.

All things bear token of decay or death,
As if our world receded from the sun,
And from the lambent spheres of life and love,
Into the fathomless and frozen void ;
And might, perchance, become a wandering orb
Sprung tangent from its bright primeval path :
A chaos habited by glimmering shapes,
Where fire had lost its heat, and light was shade,
Where sounds were echoes only, and the souls
Of living men were ghosts—and thoughts were dreams—
And Life a Picture that but seemed to live.

But lo! at signal given by Him, to whom
The axial lines round which the stars revolve
Are merely threads, His mighty hand has woven
Into the frame of Nature—lo! it turns,
And like the homeward-bending prodigal,
It nears the radiant palace of the sun,
To be re-welcomed with paternal kiss,
Re-clad in gold and purple, re-illumed
With light, and love, and joy!

Who ever sat
Contemplating on solitary hills
Beneath a canopy of cold, gray cloud,
Mantled 'gainst Northern winds, and never felt
The holy presence of invisible powers,
Nor could distinguish with attentive ear
Voices on either hand? From deep ravines,
Fainter than rustling of their own dry leaves,
Come the last quavers of the harvest song,
Which Autumn reapers sang amid their fields
Golden with sunlight—while from greenest meads
And azure vistas, shadowy, remote,
The fairy bugle of the frolic Spring,

Calling the bright-eyed flowers around her feet,
Echoes like water rippling in a dream.

Thus oscillates the mighty weight of Time
Forwards and backwards on our human hearts,
Counting our lives out with its solemn beat,
A pendulum of Memory and Hope.

THE GRAVEYARD.

THE waning light of Summer day
  Still lingers on the verdant ground,
As loth to draw its beam away
  From graven stone and grassy mound.

No voice of living Nature grieves
  For those who now for ever rest,
Nought but a sigh of rustling leaves,
  As soft as sigh from human breast.

Here let our willing feet remain,
  Nor all the busy world regret,
Whilst we enjoy that hour again
  Which all have known and all forget ;

That hour when those we call the Dead
  Come to our hearts from other spheres,
And calm delight and solace shed
  Too deep for words, too pure for tears.

Who can bewail this mortal state,
  Or question Heaven, or curse our lot,
Or e'en lament our transient date,
  In Nature's sweetest, humblest spot ?

Does not an inward teacher say
  That Death has stored no trophies here?
For angel hands have rolled away
  The stone from every sepulcher.

They all have risen ! These buried bones
  Of dust were wrought, to dust are given ;
The names upon these sculptured stones,
  Are names of those who live in Heaven.

The grandsire from his honored bier
  Arose to share immortal youth,
With kindred souls from every sphere,
  Who lived for Goodness and for Truth.

The beauteous child, by gentle powers,
  Was disentangled from his clay,
And borne to grow in heavenly bowers,
  To perfect form in perfect day.

Wife, husband, children met again,
  And in the glow of mutual love
Found all their lives, except the pain,
  Restored, renewed and blest above.

And knew ye of a constant pair
  Whose separation Fate decreed,
Whose fruitless loves were writ in air,
  Whose constant hearts were made to bleed?

Beyond this realm of hopes and dreams,
  Beneath a happier, brighter sun,
Their Spirits, like two radiant streams,
  Approached and mingled into one.

Of all the erring, base, or proud,
  If one in this fair spot there lies,
Shall we presume to pierce the cloud
  Which veils his future destinies?

Ah ! no—we never can foretell
  What fates to sinful men befall,
But this we know, and feel it well,
  Our Father made and loves them all !

With spirits strengthen'd by the Past,
  To future life we meekly turn,
While golden clouds are paling fast,
  And evening weeps at sunset's urn.

NEW THANATOPSIS.

Beneath the glory of a brighter Sun
Than that which keeps this moving globe of earth
True to its orbit, and with vision born
Of spiritual life and wisdom given of God,
I sought for Death throughout the Universe,
If haply I might note the dreaded Being
Who casts such shadows on the human heart
And breaks with his discordant string, abrupt,
The harmonies of Nature. But in vain
I scanned the range of being infinite,
From God to angels and through men to earth,
To beast, bird, serpent, and the ocean tribes,
To worms, and flowers, and the atomic forms
Of crystalline creations. Change had been,

Perpetual evolution and fresh life,
And metamorphoses to higher states,
An orderly progress, like the building up
Of pyramids from earth's material base
Into the fields of sunlight—but no Death.

With deep solemnity akin to fear
I pondered o'er the elemental world,
That seeming chaos—but its bosom held
Nought but the embryonic forms of Life.
Nor did the ideal basis of all things,
To the keen sense of spirit, elude pursuit
In chemic transformations. Then I read
The geologic leaves of stone sublime
And spiritual mysteries of primal date,
Immortal book in an immortal tongue,
Decipherable only by the light
Of a new revelation. Next I looked
Into the dark mausoleums of the Past,
And up the silent, shadowy stream of Time,
Upon whose banks nations and men, like leaves,
Lie withered. And I turned the teeming soil
Of all the battle-fields of every age;
Peered into charnels, tracked the desolate paths

Of plague and famine, and surveyed with awe
The secrets of the sea—but saw no Death.
To Spirits, the veil of whose material temple
Is rent in twain, and who are capable
Of purer thought and elemental life,
His name and nature were alike unknown.
Throughout the choral harmony of things,
And all the vast economy of God,
He had no place or office—He was not.

Then as the Sun distills vitality
Into the plastic fibers of the flower,
I felt the influx of creative Light,
Which is the heaven-sent wisdom of the mind,
And saw by intuitions not my own
The rays of Truth illumine what was dark,
And brighten what was sad before. I learned
That God alone is Life, and all our life
From him derived, and what we fancy Death
But the negation of his sacred gift,
As cold of heat, and darkness is of light.
Insensate matter is the base of all,
The footstool of our life, the supple mold
Through which the living currents come and go.

This body is the garment of the Soul,
The coarse, material outbirth of its life,
Its medium for a time, the shell which keeps
Within its curves the music of the sea,
The word expressive of the hidden thought,
A wondrous thing! which seems to live but does not,
For nothing lives but God, and we in Him.

The Spirit is a substance, a pure form
Of immaterial tissue, finely wrought
Into the human shape, unseen in this
Our physical existence, but the cause
Of all its motions, and its very life.
When ripened for a more exalted sphere,
The soul exuves this earthly envelope,
And leaves the atoms of its chemic dross
For worms, or weeds, or flowers to habit in,
While it withdraws to more august abodes,
And wakes to consciousness of deeper Life.

The Human Form receives its gift divine
In three degrees, distinct and yet united;
The Angel lives potential in the Spirit,
And both are grafted in the Natural Man,

As creatures of rare beauty lie encased
In the poor figure of an humble worm.
We move awhile in this material sphere
And form the basis of our higher life—
Celestial superstructure. God withdraws,
At his own time, the breath of his support
From this, the lowest phasis of our being,
And then we *seem* to die; but while our friends
In grief and mental blindness mourn our loss,
We have ascended to serener heights
And found a fuller and more blissful life,
Happier beyond comparison than those
Who pass in joy from hovels all forlorn
To palaces imperial.

None have died
From earth's first revolution to the present:
But all are living in congenial spheres,
And in eternal progress, in the realms
Of spiritual existence. All is Life—
Earth has indeed no monuments of death,
But only vestiges of those who passed
From this hereditary vale of shadows,
The echoes of their voices and the prints

Left by the travelers on the sands of Time.
In gloom and darkness does the Poet sing
Who calls this earth the mighty tomb of man.
'T is but his temporary habitation,
Along whose walls and silent corridors,
When he departs to more sublime abodes,
He leaves some trivial traces of himself.
The grave has nothing it can render back;
We do not pass from nature to the grave,
But Nature *is* our grave, from which we mount
At seeming death, our real resurrection,
Into the blest empyrean. And the tomb,
With all its grief, and tenderness, and shadow,
Is the creation of our sluggish minds,
By kindly memories and sweet suggestions,
To cherish and prolong the names of friends,
Gone, but not lost, unseen, but nearer still
In beauty and in glory to our life,
Which lies embedded in this natural form
Like jewel in its casket.

"Whence," I cried,
Questioning in pain my more interior mind,
"Whence then the darkness and the apprehension,

The doubt, the gloom, the fear, the agony
Of natural dissolution, which but breaks
The spell of evil and reveals to us
The inner splendors of the universe?
Why should immortal man, the image of God,
Shrink from the Jordan's pure and luminous
wave,
Whose easy passage leads him in all joy
From desert wilds to loved Jerusalem?"

Then rose a Picture representative
(The spiritual mode of teaching) to my eye.
O'er the wide world a massive shadow hung,
Blacker than winter cloud, or lonely tarn
In mountain gorges blacker e'en than night
With all its silence, and it swayed in storm
Athwart the sky and hid the glorious sun.
Darkness lay brooding on the minds of men,
And through the mists of error all they saw
Was hideous, maimed, distorted and deformed.
Foul exhalation from the sinful race,
Did Evil thus shut out the Life of God,
And the poor victims in the fearful gloom
Groaned for a quick deliv'rance. While I looked,

And grieved and wondered whence could come the
 Power
To rend and dissipate so thick a night,
The mighty shadows slowly paled away
Like loose-woven clouds dissolving into air ;
They paled away, nor left a trace behind ;
They paled away, and in their stead came Light
As of a million suns in unison,
Instinct with wondrous motions like a sea
Of golden ether, without shore or bottom,
A luminous abyss. It represented
To my touched heart the Infinite Love of God,
Which is the Life of the whole universe :
At which supernal vision I was bowed
In awe and peace and reverential joy.

L'ENVOI.

Go forth, my little Verses! to the world,
On loving errand of benignant use:
Like bees which gather up the hearts of flowers,
Like flowers which shed their fragrance on the
winds,
Like winds which bring with them the fleecy clouds,
Like clouds which are the quivers of the light,
Like rays of light new falling from the sun,
The children and the prophecies of heaven.
Go forth like these, O Verses! to the world,
And if, like these, ye glad some human heart,
And breathe into some bright expectant soul
A sense of beauty, or a thought of love
Which was not there before, I am content,
And shall receive more pleasure than I give.

IVY CLIFF.

A POEM.

IVY CLIFF.

How bright to Memory's reverted eyes
Thy happy scenes, O Ivy Cliff! arise.
O Ivy Cliff! serene and beauteous spot,
Remembered when all others are forgot,
Not as thou art do I survey thee now,
The magic rose-light faded from thy brow,
Music no longer echoing in thy glen,
(The pearls of childhood are but stones to men,)
But as thou wert in life's delightful morn,
When from thy side I heard the fairy's horn;
And dreamed that dream which once to all is
given,
Of Jacob's ladder reaching into heaven.

A beetling bluff, with ivy overgrown,
Chos'n from its sister-hills and loved alone,
Dew-crowned at morning lured my step away,
With noontide calm solicited my stay,
With evening beauties made me linger still
Till purple twilight darkened all the hill;
Its mantled front with brownest shade replete,
A voiceless river winding at its feet.
Pent up by hills in ever-during thrall,
The deep, dark water scarcely moved at all,
But, uncomplaining of its rocky chain,
Lay like a Titan, silent in his pain.

The rugged sides of Ivy Cliff were hung
With waving branches, ever green and young,
A sylvan labyrinth of light and shade
By clambering vines and blended bushes made;
A living wall of vegetable birth;
A shining vesture o'er the granite earth.
When the flowers perished and the waters
froze,
Throughout the melancholy waste of snows,
Sweetly it beamed upon the gladdened eye,
Emblem of Hope and Truth which never die.

Near the bold summit burst a spring to view
Colder than night and brighter than its dew.
Briefly through moss the little rivulet ran
Bound, like an infant-life, to narrow span,
Fell o'er the rocks, with transitory gleam,
And perished weeping in the larger stream.
It seemed to me the Spirit of the Hill
Voiced and embodied as a flowing rill,
Whispering to unseen listeners of its own
Sorrows and joys, alike to us unknown;
For sometimes it would strangely change its sound
When not a leaf or wave was moving round.
When wintry voices echoed wailing by,
And every breeze was Nature's wingéd sigh,
The brook would sing upon its joyous way
Like bright-eyed boy upon a holiday.
Again when Summer had reclad the earth,
And all the air was redolent with mirth,
With hum of bees and wings of butterflies,
With lay of birds and airy symphonies,
The brook, with feeble murmur of its fall,
Sent alien sounds of sadness o'er them all!

O! sweet it was on early Summer morn
From Ivy Cliff to hear the hunter's horn,
With skillful quaver all the forest fill,
Ere yet the Sun had kissed the eastern hill,
Burst on the air of dewy solitudes
And break the stillness of the dreaming woods,
Then die away in distance from the ear
Where none but hare or startled fox could hear;
And when the sun, o'er boundless field of light,
Rolling his chariot to triumphal height,
Shot down the valleys many a piercing ray,
And broke the rolls of silver mist away,
The passing boatman gave his wild halloo,
The startled hawk returned it as he flew,
The wood subdued it to a lengthened moan,
And Echo murmured from her couch of stone.

There had my boyhood chosen—who has not?
For lonelier hours a sweet and silent spot,
From all the tumult of the world remote,
Where I could steal when none would care or note;
Like a lone cloud which softly breaks away
From all the dark tempestuous array,

And floats far off in sunny joy to lie
O'er sleeping seas in fields of azure sky.

On Ivy Cliff beneath the kindly shade,
When heaven was bright and all the winds were
laid,
With summer beauty glowing all around,
With rural ease and quietness profound,
With purple mountains fading into blue,
And Otter's ever-radiant peaks in view ;
With all we wish in water, earth, or sky,
To please the mind and to delight the eye ;
I read and loved the bards of former age,
Milton's great song and Spencer's sweetest page.
Nor did I care though warblers in the green
Allured me sweetly from the "Fairy Queen ;"
Nor though some cloud-built palace won mine eyes
From the bright scenes in Adam's paradise,
The soft transition was with joy replete,
The soft return to Poësy as sweet ;
Mere changes in the notes, which all belong
To one great choral harmony of song.
There often lost in reverie would I lie,
Till the last gleams were fading from the sky,

Till the last echo of Heaven's gate of gold
Closing in music o'er the ether rolled,
Then lingering in the weird and waning light,
My fancy would transform, on neighboring height,
The dim-seen branches of some towering tree
To giant knight of Paynim chivalry.

Men, books and nature mold the growing mind,
And each a deep impression leaves behind
Nor Time, nor Circumstance can e'er efface,
Which curious eyes in after years may trace.
When with the school my studious hours began,
I leaned to Nature rather than to man—
And still I turn from all that Man has wrought
To Nature for my sweetest hours of thought:
For plastic Nature's busy atoms move
Obedient to impulses from above;
Thus picturing forth the mysteries which lie
Beyond the range of our material eye:
A speech of things, not words, by which are given
Thoughts and emotions which have come from
heaven;
That speech whereby since solar time began
The unseen Angels have conversed with man.

O Ivy Cliff! with robes of evergreen,
With many a Spring and many a Summer scene,
With all the soft, the beautiful, the bright,
In subtlest tissues of ethereal light,
Didst thou not shed upon my soul a power
Unfelt as sunbeams by the growing flower,
Feeding in secret my too hopeful heart
With the great thoughts whose hieroglyph thou wert?
And thou, Dark River! with unchanging form,
Silent and strong in sunshine or in storm,
Locked in thy hills, like prisoner of state,
Didst thou not make me braver for my fate?
O Wizard Wind! that wanderest unseen
Athwart the hills or down the deep ravine,
With every note of gladness or of grief
Which hails the bred or weeps the falling leaf,
Hast thou not breathed upon my lyre, unknown,
When all believed the numbers were my own?
And ye, Belovéd Mountains! which arise
Silently cleaving the eternal skies,
Ye raised my Spirit to an atmosphere
Of peace and beauty, above mortal care;

Ye made me yearn in loftier degree
For mental than for natural liberty,
Aspire to climb the mountains of the Mind,
And leave the laggards of the age behind;
Stand in the sunlight on the mighty brow,
Nor heed the pigmies who might mock below!

When draws the festal month of Childhood near,
"The merriest, maddest time of all the year,"
When rosy school-girls count the hours away,
In sweet anticipation of the day,
The willing boys their little labors share,
And to the Cliff in eager troop repair,
For gay festoons of graceful evergreen
To deck the palace of the May-day Queen.
Sad havoc make the busy urchins there,
While jocund laughter shakes the genial air;
Voices and echoes leave no pause between,
And the glad sunshine animates the scene.
Loud crack the branches as the best are culled,
Till every hand a weighty load has pulled.
The task fulfilled, they all relax their powers,
Some hie to play, and some in search of flowers,

To catch the heart's-ease nodding by the brook,
Or steal the violet from its shaded nook.
Some careless loll upon the shining grass
And watch the clouds and shadows as they pass;
While some heave mighty stones adown the steep
Into the sluggish water dark and deep,
Admire the plunge and watch the circling ray,
And hear the muffled echoes roll away.
The birds in terror shun their green retreat,
And Silence routed flies his favorite seat,
Like a stern eagle winging from his woods
To loneliest tarn in mountain solitudes.
At length accloyed with pleasure's sweet excess,
For ah! our hearts can tire of happiness!
They bear their treasures to the busy girls
Chattering mid golden locks or raven curls;
The kind assistance smiling lips repay,
And bright eyes speak what lips could never say!

But ah! why does the echo of my lyre
From such gay theme in trembling wail expire?
As if some Sunbeam on my life had shed
Its power, and left a Shadow in its stead;

As if some Joy from out my heart had flown
And left a weeping Memory there alone.
Oh yes! there is a spot for sacred tears,
A green, green mound which early love endears.
Rainbows would arch it with eternal glow,
And Angels guard it—if she slept below;
But jewel-crowned, white-vestured, harp in hand,
She has arisen into the Morning Land.
Before her eyes supernal glories shine,
As radiant as she made the world to mine;
And seraph voices in that realm she hears
As raptly as I listened once to hers.
She was the fairest of the May-day Queens,
And I the happiest in those woodland scenes;
O'er fields of bleak December still I stray,
All radiant she in her eternal May!

Spring-times and Summers of the rolling year!
Why come ye back with your prolific cheer?
Shadows and Memories ye can e'er restore,
The Joys, the Sunbeams, ye can bring no more!

O Love! Young Love! Thou dear Divinity!
What happy worship have I rendered thee;

What hopes, what sighs, what dreams I can recall,
What fears, what ecstasies! Thou hadst them all!
Yet was devotion with such bounty paid,
Sò heavenly sweet was ardent service made,
No vow was uttered which I could regret,
No pang was felt, but I would feel it yet.

Thou, Ivy Cliff! hast witnessed how I loved,
And with responsive tenderness approved;
For Nature to the Poet's heart reveals
In her bright forms the sympathy she feels.
How clear the young birds caroled round my
seat,
How fresh the ivy glistened at my feet,
How soft the zephyrs sighed upon the air,
How sweet the ringdove's cooing murmur there,
How beautiful the clouds, as if they wove
Ethereal palaces for dreaming Love,
Whilst pensive lay the shadowy stream below
Touched as with joy by evening's purple glow!
Thus didst thou, Nature! with complying art
Echo the subtle passion of my heart,
In outward forms renew my joys again,
And nurse in secret my delightful pain.

At the soft close of cheerful summer day,
When golden clouds were fading into gray,
When the rich purple deepened on the hill,
And the dark river became darker still,
Whilst in the twilight's azure field afar
The new moon hung her silver scimitar,
Oft have I paused on Ivy Cliff to hear
A homely music echoing far and near ;
The Negro reapers, singing as they went,
A homeward burst of native merriment,
Which seemed to me a melancholy strain,
A wild, mixed melody of joy and pain,
Dying in sadness on the distant hill,
Lost in the call of lonely whip-poor-will.

The painted savage, Ishmael of the West,
Insensate once this glorious soil possessed ;
Untouched by all the loveliness we see,
Unawed by Nature's dread sublimity.
The Race which neither fear nor pity knew,
No arts could soften and no arms subdue,
Fell on these hunting grounds, a stoic prey,
Or roamed to wilder hunting grounds away,

Destined at last, on far Pacific shore,
To sink from Nature's sunlight evermore.
But the poor Negro, of a gentler mind,
Obedient, peaceful, teachable and kind,
Unfit for commerce or for war's alarms,
Incapable alike of arts and arms,
Organically slow and weak and mild,
A Childlike Race, eternally a Child,
Condemned to service in his brother's tent,
Finds in that service his true element.

From golden Africa's barbaric shore,
Sold by his kinsmen, he was dragged of yore;
A naked, trembling, weeping wretch he came,
The child of superstition, blood and shame:
Redeemed forever from his moral night,
To useful labors gently trained aright,
In just subordination, wisely led,
Subservient as the hand is to the head,
With thought and feeling kindling on his brow
From a new life transfused, behold him now!
By full provision and protection here,
By justice, mercy, and by loving care,

By the great light which civilization spreads,
And by the blessings which Religion sheds,
We give him, delving in the sun and soil,
A fair remuneration for his toil.
For names not principles let fools contend,
We see the methods, Providence the end:
The slave may be a freeman in his chain,
Bonds may be broken and the slave remain;
One truth is clear: *The Good alone are free,*
And mutual service is true Liberty!

One of those slumbrous, hazy Autumn eves,
When the old forest dropt his crimson leaves,
Twirling and rustling softly to the ground
With a remote and melancholy sound,
From Ivy Cliff I pensively surveyed
The gradual changes which decay had made.
From its cold fount the little rivulet wept,
And o'er its path with feeble murmur crept,
Soon to be hush'd in every frozen wave,
Like Moorish statue in enchanted cave,
In fixed forgetfulness or silent pain
Until the Spring dissolved the spell again.

On the chill air broke forth a joyful breeze,
Last relic of the Summer symphonies,
But was death-stricken to a pause—and then,
Ghost of itself, went wailing down the glen.
There as I mused, a sweet and subtle Power
Smote on my heart, like sunbeams on the flower;
As if some Spirit which had been a-glow
In Spring or Summer had refused to go
To the embrace of Winter, drear and cold,
And passed into a heart of human mold.
Straightway I sighed with an ambitious hope
To draw from Nature's great kaleidoscope
Some form of thought which would not soon expire,
Some living note to vibrate from my lyre,
And waft away o'er hearts and homes afar
The light, the love, the blessing of a star.
Thus from the wreck the seasons leave behind
We may distill new vigor of the mind;
As strength is born of melancholy hours,
Or sweetest odors come from wounded flowers,
As Hope relumes the ashes of Despair,
Or violets starting from our graves appear.

When Ivy Cliff was mantled all in snow,
And frolic skaters on the stream below
Sent jovial voices on the Northern breeze,
And tinkling echoes whistling through the trees,
On the bleak hill I paid my last adieu
To scenes the dearest which my childhood knew.

A wondrous city in the West appeared,
On hills of amber and of pearl upreared;
Commingling shone its palaces afar,
Each dome a sun, each pointing spire a star;
Glowing it stretched beyond the visual powers,
And sapphire canopy o'erhung its towers.
When lo! as softly as a breaking dream,
Or bright reflection wavering in a stream,
They parted, spires, domes, towers and turrets all,
Like a great realm dissolving to its fall;
The splendid fragments faded on the wind,
Nor left to night one radiant trace behind.

When from the scene my tardy footstep turned.
A new ambition in my spirit burned—
To do some deed according to my power,
If Heaven would give the means and send the hour,

Which in the lapse of Time should bear its part
T' illume the mind and cheer the human heart.
Majestic rivers gliding to their goal
Give life and wealth to nations as they roll,
The humblest flower that e'er exhales the dew
Leaves on the earth its little blessing too.
Vain are the labors and the schemes of man
Unless accordant with the Eternal Plan ;
Uncheered by light from brighter sun than ours
We waste our thoughts, we desecrate our powers.
In works of mind and in affairs of state
They are serenely wise and truly great,
And they alone, who bring us from above,
Some ray of Truth, some spark of heavenly Love.

AGATHE.

A TRAGEDY IN TWO ACTS.

DRAMATIS PERSONÆ.

LYCANDER....A Grecian King, just returned from Troy.

THERON......A Military Attendant.

CHRESTUS.....Friend of Theron, Guardian of Elpenor and Agathe.

ELPENOR.....Nephew to Lycander—and the rightful King.

AGATHE......Priestess of Diana's Temple and Sister to Elpenor.

ACT I.

SCENE I.

A Private Garden.—Chrestus and Theron.

Chrestus.

So happy have I been, belovéd Theron!
In the repeated welcomes of my heart
To thee and all, that for this one bright hour,
Sole one for many years! I have forgotten
The mighty shadow gathering o'er our lives,
And the dread secret which we two have kept
So long in pain, unshared. How fares the King?

Theron.

As such a man should fare: his visions haunt him
With ten-fold power. At first he was but sad
And spent whole days in moping reverie,
Losing all sense of pleasure in the chase,

In music, feasting, or the pomp of state,
In man or soothing woman. This had happened
Before we parted. Then came fearful dreams,
And sudden, terrible wakings in the night,
Which made his eye grow wild and his face pale
And stern and haggard ; afterwards appeared
Mysterious visions, phantasies, no doubt,
Of a mind conscience-stricken and appalled
By the foreshadowings of its doom ; at last
The unsubstantial images of thought
Took form and shape as palpable to sense
As things of earth. With e'er-increasing power,
Exciting fear sometimes almost to agony,
They broke upon his revels and his sleep,
Peopled his tent and dogged his chariot wheels.

CHRESTUS.

Do these illusions ever intimate,
By special uniformity of type,
The nature of his guilt ?

THERON.

He never tells
By words explicit what he hears or sees ;
But, from expressions dropped in quick surprise,

Wild exclamations made in sudden fear,
And mutterings when he thought himself alone,
I find the central figure of the group
In all his dreams or waking phantasies
Is that dead brother, whose great crown he wears,
Unfortunate Elpenor, whom he pushed,
One hunting day, from a wild precipice,
And made the world believe, except us two,
It was an accident.

CHRESTUS.

In all his ravings
Speaks he ever of the children?

THERON.

No, never.
He thinks them dead.

CHRESTUS.

'T is well indeed he does!
And may he never know the truth, unless
Some sweet compunction of relenting nature
Impel his soul to righteous restitution.
Yet it is strange the secret, dread remembrance
Of murdered innocence should not oppress him.

Is crime by proxy less a crime than that
We do with our own hands? What's to be done?

THERON.

He has dispatched a trusty messenger
To Jupiter's great Oracle of Dodona,
And the response is momently expected.

CHRESTUS.

I have no faith or hope that any answer,
Or sage advice or solemn prophecy,
Can ever turn his footsteps back again
To the old, happy path he has deserted.

THERON.

Then, Chrestus! what is left but revolution?
All hate his rule—yea, even fear his voice,
And scowl upon him as he passes by
In his abstracted moods. None dare approach him
Or seem to mark him when the fit is on.
His temper has become morose and fierce,
Fiery, inconstant, and tyrannical.
These traits were serviceable whilst they made him
Invincible in battle. But at home,
When slaughtered Trojans can not give his spleen

A bloody vent and calm his demon rage,
Wherever he shall turn his baleful eye
Some curse or sad calamity impends.
I fear to think upon the state of things
We may expect.

CHRESTUS.

O Theron! when the Gods,
In dreadful chastisement of human sin,
Have pushed their victim to the furthest verge
Of madness, men in righteous self-defense
May consummate the sentence. It was well
This dark-soul'd fratricide took off with him
The turbulent spirits of our realm to Troy.
He served the common cause; he was the tool
Of Grecian glory, leaving us at home
Ten years of prosperous peace. Sweet Agathe,
Reared in the temple of our chaste Diana,
Unfolded to each new admiring summer
Her pure and radiant graces for our joy,
Herself almost a Goddess. Elpenor grew
Meanwhile from boyhood to that golden age
When life and hope are brightest. If Lycander
Has reached the limit of his fatal chain,

'T is time to strike; a worthier hand is ready
To grasp the scepter. But let nothing rash,
No vulgar rage, no impulse of revenge,
Stain the pure power and virtuous dignity
Whereby our human hands co-work with heaven.
Leave him alone awhile, for if I read
Aright the deep philosophy of Fate
His hands unconsciously will weave the web
To tangle his own feet. Go through the city
And test the opinions of the populace
On his return. Myself will seek his palace,
And see which way the wind lies; if it promise
Propitious calm, or bode such coming storm
As must subside in human wreck and woe.

[*Exeunt.*

SCENE II.

TEMPLE OF DIANA.—AGATHE ALONE.

DREAMS which escape the memory may leave
Their melancholy traces on the soul;
Else why should now a vague presentiment
Of coming evil fall upon my heart,

Like the slow shadow of a pendent cloud
Upon the plain beneath? My only friends,
The dear Elpenor and our noble Chrestus
Are well and happy. The common heart of Greece
Is joyous at our army's safe return,
And beauty hastes to join her tender rose
To the majestic laurel. What should I fear?
Alas! no sorrow can disturb the good:
Cares nestle only in the wicked breast.
O chaste Diana! whose exalting presence
Is brighter, purer, dearer to the soul
Than thine own moon, at fullest, to the world;
Here let me consecrate myself anew,
Heart, mind and body to thy holy service,
And so escape the power of evil thoughts!

[*Enter* ELPENOR.

ELPENOR.

Forever wrapt in pious meditation,
Sweet Agathe! Hast thou no voice of praise
For deeds heroic, no free and sunny smile
For Grecian triumph?

AGATHE.

Yes—for Grecian triumph,
And tears for Trojan woes. O that our warriors

Had left such full and happy homes behind them
As greet them here!

ELPENOR.

What were the glory then
Without the charm of danger? What the toil
Of war without the bloodshed of our foes?
The ten-year's siege is over; Troy has fallen;
And the long blaze of military splendors
Lives only now in song, unparalleled
By aught that was before or ever shall be.
Alas! that I too was not earlier born!
Oh! I remember, as 't were yesterday,
That glorious morning when the gay-decked fleet
Swung at loose anchor on the shining bay.
The bright-plumed warriors rowed toward their
ships
With music and the stroke of thousand oars
In thrilling unison. Their glowing armor,
As yet undented by the Trojan steel,
Flashed in the sun. Their parting shout of cheer
Startled the echoes of the wooded hills.
Thousands were crowded on the curving shore
And waved their last adieu. When the far ships

Stood boldly out towards the fretful sea,
The mighty multitude in groups retired ;
But yet I lingered, till the setting sun
Gleamed faintly from the last receding sail,
And dropped my tears upon the yellow beach
That I was not a soldier.

AGATHE.

Foolish boy !
Insensate to the unrecorded griefs
Of our forlorn humanity.

ELPENOR.

When I
Come glorying homeward from some foreign war,
And shouting citizens in exultation
Draw me triumphant through the living streets,
My Agathe will meet me with a tear,
And turn her gentle eyes away, forsooth,
Because my hands were gory.

AGATHE.

No more war !
Is not the earth now drunk with human blood ?
Ah ! turn thy face upon the golden grain

Waving continuous from field to field ;
On pleasant cottages embowered in trees ;
On herds and flocks, and children's merry play ;
On rivulets leaping in the summer sun
Through emerald meadows ; on the social gleam
Of towers and towns along the winding bay :—

ELPENOR.

Hold, hold—I can admire thy brilliant pictures,
But, sweetest Sister ! sage Philosophy,
And e'en benign Religion, sanction war
When savage men conspire against our rights
And break our peace.

AGATHE.

But ah ! the time approaches
When sated Strife shall sheathe his crimson steel,
And every soul partake the mutual glow
In which the loving sun would bind us all.
Look at the stars upon a cloudless night !
Shining they move in circles which we know not,
Making eternal music as they go :
Undimmed and undisturbed, countless in number,
They never jostle and they never fade.

In such array shall human hearts combine,
And in the order and the peace of heaven
Regenerate the earth.

ELPENOR.

Fair prophetess!
If our old heroes could but hear thy song
They might cast off their mail and splendid helms,
And hie contented to some mountain-side,
To play the Doric reed and pasture sheep.

AGATHE.

Thou ever turn'st my earnestness to sport.

ELPENOR.

Then, not to sport—A low, portentous cloud,
Just o'er the distant hill-tops swiftly risen,
Comes darkening on apace. Suspicion, fear,
And discontent are lowering on the brows
Of soldiery and people. Some affirm
The king is mad—

AGATHE.

The king is mad? Alas!

ELPENOR.

Dark rumors are afloat of usurpation,
Startling the city into wild surprise,
And hurried whispers—with still darker hints
Of coming revolution ; what to look for
Men know not.

AGATHE.

O my sad, prophetic heart !

ELPENOR.

What truth is in it all, what falsity,
What source is claimed, what issues are involved,
I can not tell, all—all is dark as yet.
But I would hold my spirit well prepared ;
And so I come with offerings to our Goddess,
To beg her favor and her wise protection,
To keep my heart serene amid all tumult,
My judgment clear, my loyalty to truth,
My love of country unimpeachable.
I would not draw my sword but for true cause,
And having drawn it, would not put it up
Till Mercy bids and Justice shall approve.

AGATHE.

Bravely and wisely spoken, my good brother !
Minerva smiles when Mars relenting wreathes
His sword-hilt with the gracious olive branch.
Go quickly ! meet me at the sacred altar ;
I will array in white and deck with flowers,
And we will offer up a lamb, in token
Of our pure motives and the peace we sigh for.

[*Exit* ELPENOR.

He too is sad ! Ah ! now I understand
The melancholy mood which came o'er me
By spiritual contagion. Far apart
Their bodies may be, but the souls of those
Who love are never sundered. I remember
One summer evening, at the very moment
When he was drowning in the boiling surf,
(But Chrestus plucked him from the watery grave),
A chill of terror crept into my heart,
Far in the secret chambers of the temple.
The King is mad ; the people discontented ;
Truly the shadow deepens !

[*Exit.*

SCENE III.

Room in the Palace of the King.—Lycander alone.

Lycander.

I ne'er believed that things impalpable
Could locate like the fixtures of a room,
And haunt the eye with their continual presence;
Closed or unclosed I see him. I have tried
Every expedient to appease this fierce
Offended shade, and deprecate his wrath;
Have offered wine and fruits upon his grave,
And a whole hecatomb of living creatures.
Prayers, tears, and protestations of remorse
Have proved alike in vain. I now await
The issue of another measure.

[*Knocking is heard.*]

Who knocks?

At first I started up at every noise,
Like the scared wild deer in his leafy lair;
But I have learned, by constant observation,
The ghastly images which haunt my steps

Are voiceless. I am not afraid of sounds.
Come in.

[*Enter* CHRESTUS.

CHRESTUS.

Great King! thy orders are obeyed.

LYCANDER.

Hast thou o'erturned the accursèd monument
And ploughed the ground whereon its stones were reared?
Hast thou destroyed the great ancestral urn
And strewed the royal ashes on the sea?

CHRESTUS.

Thou art obeyed!

LYCANDER.

Thou mock'st me, lying Chrestus!
The monument still stands; the urn retains
Its untouched treasure in the old repose.
I see thou askest with indignant eyes
Why I should question thy veracity.
The spirits of the dead cling to the spots
Which hold their ashes. Move but these away
And the complying shadows follow. This,

Hadst thou obeyed my mandate to the letter,
This nightmare of my life, like some poor dream,
Had now departed. Look into that corner!

CHRESTUS.

Where? What? Unhappy monarch! I see nothing.

LYCANDER.

Dost thou not see that wretched, bleeding man,
Lying nearly prostrate underneath the rock?
His body writhes in mortal agony,
With every muscle from its natural line
Protruded and contorted, in the vain
But unremitting struggle to arise.
Canst thou not read the language of that face,
Fear, torture, mute reproaches, and surprise?
Ha! ha! Too well thou know'st it is my brother!

CHRESTUS.

Indeed I have seen nothing. It must be
Some dreadful picture which was once impressed
Too strongly on thy memory, and comes
Back in reverberation of the light,
Like sounds in echo.

LYCANDER.

Slave! wouldst thou reproach me
With irrevocable calamities?
I should have silenced thee in time.

[*Knocking.*

What now?
What other spy upon my misery?

[*Enter* THERON.

Speak briefly, villain! hast thou come to join
This suborned witness in his perjury?

THERON.

I simply come to give thee the response
Of the great Oracle of Jupiter
In this sealed package.

LYCANDER.

Let me have it quickly:
Grant me, ye Gods! one gleam of consolation!
Is mystery solved by mystery? What is this?

[*Reads aloud.*

"*He who would satisfy the injured dead*
Must put the crown upon the living head."

The living head? what 's this? what living head?
Theron and Chrestus, I command ye here,
Great sages that ye are, to read me promptly,
On pain of instant death, this Jovian riddle.
What living head is this of which he speaks?
How! Are ye silent? Are ye struck with dumbness
In punishment of some great treachery?
Or are ye pausing to concoct a sly
And sure equivocation?

THERON.

O, Lycander!
The children thou commanded'st me to kill
I gave to Chrestus.

CHRESTUS.

And I spared their lives,
Rearing them for the service of the state,
And to secure thee in thy last distress,
Unhappy fratricide! a hope of mercy
By a late restitution. Thank us truly
For this most pious fraud. Why dost thou glare,
Gasping for breath?

LYCANDER.

Away !

THERON.

Hear me, Lycander !

LYCANDER.

Nay, traitors ! not a word—now, list my will !
Bring me these children in three hours, or you
And they, and all that aid you or abet,
Shall perish by the sword ! Quick, from my sight !

[*Exeunt* CHRESTUS AND THERON.

They live ! Ah ! now I clearly see the cause
Why my dead brother can not find repose
Beyond the ever dark and silent river.
This oracle would lead me to my ruin.
Restore the crown ? such weakness leave for fools !
I will dispatch the living to the dead
And so appease his rage—or not at all.
Ha ! dost thou frown, inevitable shadow ?
Frown on, dread phantom ! Canst thou stay my
arm ?

[*Exit* LYCANDER.

SCENE IV.

GROVE IN FRONT OF DIANA'S TEMPLE.—AGATHE AND CHRESTUS.

AGATHE.

GOOD Chrestus! why so stern and melancholy,
Haste in thy steps, and frowns upon thy brow?
Would I had met thee in a brighter mood!
I have a small petition to prefer,
And can not bear denial from thy lips.

CHRESTUS.

Or sad or gay did ever I refuse
A boon to Agathe?

AGATHE.

Nay, thou art kind,
And never did my mind misgive till now;
But this concerns the King. Why start'st thou so
At the mere name of King?

CHRESTUS.

The King, Lycander?

What know'st thou of the King? Better it were
Thou never hadst been born than meet that King.

AGATHE.

Chrestus! his miseries have touched my heart.
He is disquieted in mind and body,
His strength is failing and his sleep is broken
By fearful visions.

CHRESTUS.

Know'st thou his disease?

AGATHE.

Ten weary years of fierce, continuous war,
Absence from home, privation and fatigue,
The unremitting labors of the mind,
Thirst, hunger, wounds, the torture of defeat,
The more convulsing rage of victory,
The scenes of carnage and perpetual riot,
Might well occasion any mortal ill,
E'en to the verge of madness.

CHRESTUS.

Wide the mark!
O Agathe! the king is mad, if madness

Be not too mild a term for a blind frenzy,
With conscience for the torturer.

AGATHE.

Alas!
What hath he done?

CHRESTUS.

Done? Ancient deeds of crime,
Which innocent and happy men forget,
But which grow brighter in the memories
Of those who do them.

AGATHE.

Ah! I yearn the more
To offer to the royal sufferer
With chaste and eager hand the golden cup
Of consolation. If his malady
Be spiritual, spiritual must be the means
Of restoration.

CHRESTUS.

Canst thou by persuasion
Quiet the raging waters of the deep
When they come foaming to the frighted shores?

Canst thou with charms or priestly eloquence,
Or with more potent tears and supplications,
Drive the malignant Furies from the prey
For which they howl?

AGATHE.

Not I, O no! not I,
But can the gods not do it? Dost thou doubt
The graciousness of heaven, the potency
Of sacred offerings made with holy rites,
With humble prayers and penitential vows?
O Chrestus! let this miserable King
Kneel at Diana's shrine, whilst I implore
Her blessings on his head. The ghastly forms
Will not pursue him to this sacred spot.
Here the propitious glow of heaven perchance,
Like sunshine gleaming o'er a wintry world,
May melt into his heart. He will relent!

CHRESTUS.

Sweet Agathe! thou dost not know the monster
For whom thou pleadst. He is accursed of heaven,
His hand—ah, yes! his soul is stained with blood:
There is no spot unsullied in his nature.

Shall he be welcomed to these sacred groves?
Thy trees would murmur forth their discontent;
Thy doves would fly the desecrated place;
Thy flowers would fade; the statue of thy Goddess
Would tremble on its silver pedestal:
Famine or plague would scourge us for such wrong
To her divinity.

AGATHE.

Judge him not harshly.

CHRESTUS.

Harshly? Why, he slew his only brother,
Young, gallant, generous, loving, beautiful;
He slew him for his crown. And at this moment
Thyself, Elpenor, Theron, I and all
Stand in the imminent jeopardy of life
From his explosive passions. Even now
He has commanded us to drag thy brother,
And thee thyself, sweet Agathe! before him.

AGATHE.

O, wherefore, noble Chrestus? How have we
Offended him?

CHRESTUS.

Who knows? No one can tell
What desperate turn his phantasies may take.

AGATHE.

O, bring him here!

CHRESTUS.

Art thou not now afraid
To meet this tyrant?

AGATHE.

No! I say again,
Leaning upon Diana's radiant arm
For her serene protection, bring him here!
Dost thou remember on a summer eve,
Two years ago, we found an aged man
Stretched sleeping in this cool and grateful shade
From utter weariness? His beard was long,
And hunger on his frowning countenance
Had made its ghastly lines; his feet were bare;
His hair was matted with the stems and burrs
Caught in the woods; his eyeballs, shot with
blood,
Were half revealed as if he feared to sleep.

This man had killed his children, and remorse
Had wrecked his reason, while the public wrath
Banished the miscreant from the face of man.
None gave him needful fire, or food, or shelter;
All cursed him as he passed. When from his sleep
He started up, he raved, and called his children,
Like a young mother wailing for her babe,
The first-born, newly dead. I laid my hands
Upon his trembling brow, and weeping prayed
Our Goddess to befriend the poor forlorn.
Long time he gazed upon me, then he wept,
Then fell asleep again; this time he smiled
As if his dreams were pleasant. When he woke
'T was to the common light and lot of men;
His mind was rational, his spirit bowed
In penitence and fervent gratitude.
See what a child can do, if Heaven approve!
So let it be with this distracted King.

CHRESTUS.

Why waste thy sacred sympathy on a soul
Impervious to all good? This wretched King
Spun for himself the web of destiny.
The soldiers hate his savage rule; the people

Abhor his name ; he wears the crown which Nature
Gave to another. A thousand hands are ready
To pluck the stolen jewel from his brow.
Our plan is laid. We can not give him freedom
To consummate his own unhappy fall,
Involving as it might the woe of others :
But our indignant steel is leaping forth
For retribution. Why delay an hour
To test thy merciful but hopeless scheme
On such a man ?

AGATHE.

O Chrestus ! noble Chrestus !
Hast thou, who art so generous, good and wise,
And hold such close communion with the Gods,
Ere stooping to a rash conspiracy,
Hast thou accorded to this luckless King
The universal privilege of man :
Lenient construction and the amplest chance
Of reformation ? Let our sweet Religion
Weave round his human heart its holy bands.
They may withdraw him from the precipice
To which he verges. He may yet confess
His terrible transgression and appease

The anger of the Gods and men by full
And noble restitution. He may make
Some expiation of the guilty past
By an old age of honorable use.
Chrestus! good Chrestus! grant this single boon
To him—to me—and to thy generous heart.

CHRESTUS.

Well, well, so be it! I will bring him here,
And thou shalt have fair trial; but I know
Fruitless will be thy task. The twisted oak
Yields not its sturdy branches to the wind
Like the compliant willow.

AGATHE.

Thanks, O thanks!
I will prepare.

CHRESTUS.

One moment: Agathe!
I put this curious ring upon thy finger.
Note well this hidden spring, which on the touch
Shoots out a drop of subtlest poison.

AGATHE.

Poison?

CHRESTUS.

Whoever gets it on his lip or breathes it
Falls straightway helpless, breathless, and may die
If he inhales enough. Remember this.

AGATHE.

What should I do with poison?

CHRESTUS.

Keep it, child!
The man thou art to deal with is a madman,
Impetuous, cruel and ungovernable.
Thy virgin instincts might demand a weapon,
Just such as this, invisible, unfailing,
Quick in its action,—

AGATHE.

Chrestus! I am safe
Beneath the shadow of Diana's statue
From all the baleful movements of the stars,
Much more from any thing that men can do.

CHRESTUS.

Take it, sweet Agathe! and say no more;
I shall be happier thus.

AGATHE.

Then let us haste.

CHRESTUS.

Stay for a moment ; Agathe ! my child !
An ominous shadow falls upon my heart
At this consent.

AGATHE.

That false and evil shadow
Which sometimes comes o'er heaven's selected hour
To mar its sweet impression ! Let us go.
What can we dread when in our humble spheres
We meekly strive to imitate the Gods ?

[*Exeunt.*

ACT II.

SCENE I.

GARDEN OF CHRESTUS.—CHRESTUS AND THERON.

CHRESTUS.

AT first Lycander bitterly refused
To see the priestess or propitiate
Diana's favor ; and would scarcely listen
With any patience till I had confessed
That Agathe, the vestal of the temple,
Was the fair daughter of his murdered brother.
He then agreed.

THERON.

How did they meet ?

CHRESTUS.

We went,
Myself in silence, he with broken words,

Part imprecations on th' avenging shadow,
Part blasphemies against the Gods, until
We reached the green sward of the sacred grove;
When lo! the bright and gentle Agathe
Glided serenely toward us through the trees
As might the moon, with Dian for its soul,
Shine softly down the azure field of heaven
Beset with clouds. O she was beautiful!
Her radiating goodness seemed to make
A golden halo round her, which infused
Such peace into the soul one could believe
The music of Elysian bowers remote
Was lulling him to sleep. The King, amazed,
Looked wondering at her as she meekly knelt
And kissed his hand. Rising, she welcomed him
With such a radiant grace and eloquence
Of word and look, that he appeared entranced,
And mutely walked with her toward the temple.

THERON.

Think'st thou he will be softened?

CHRESTUS.

For a while;
But the old shadows will come back again.

Elpenor must be king. Hast thou revealed
The secret of his birth?

THERON.

Yes, and he heard it
Surprised indeed, but with a dignity
Which proved his soul heroic. But he vowed
Before the sun, and moon, and all the stars
To wreak upon the frenzied fratricide
A bloody and a swift revenge.

CHRESTUS.

Now see!
Nor time, nor place, nor thwarting circumstance,
Nor education, nor the power of years
Of strict seclusion, nor opposing lessons,
Can e'er extinguish in the human breast
The spark of our hereditary natures.
This youth, the scion of a martial stock,
A line of fierce, ungovernable kings,
Whose food was blood and whose delight was war,
Is ready in the twinkling of an eye
To doff the robes of philosophic ease
And wear the imperial purple.

THERON.

He will grace it :
For magnanimity subdues his pride,
Too fiery else, to a becoming luster.
He granted my request, and waits with us
To see if Agathe's sweet, plastic power
Can mold the obdurate temper of the King
To happier issues. If she shall succeed,
He spares his life and orders banishment ;
But if she fail, as fail she will, his sword
Is consecrated to its awful duty.

CHRESTUS.

Mercy and Justice both are satisfied.
All things look bright, yet, throbbing with suspense,
My heart is wretched. O sweet Agathe !
How tardily this daylight wears away !

[*Exeunt*

SCENE II.

INTERIOR OF DIANA'S TEMPLE.—LYCANDER AND AGATHE.

LYCANDER.

I WILL not leave thee, Maiden ! I will dwell
Here in this temple, ever in thy presence ;
For at thy side there's peace and blessedness ;
If thou but turn that radiant face away,
The shadows quickly gather o'er my soul,
And all is dark again. I will not leave thee !
Now by the Gods ! I will not.

AGATHE.

King Lycander !
Thy crown, thy scepter, duty's high behest—

LYCANDER.

Such plausive words of wisdom move me not ;
I 'm no philosopher. In the new joy,
New life, new heaven, which I receive from thee,
I have forgotten my imperial home,

And never care to think of it again.
Thou art my heart, my hope, my life, my all!

AGATHE.

Attribute not, O King, to a poor mortal
The gracious blessing of the pitying Gods.
This is the sanctuary of Diana,
A chaste, secluded, consecrated spot,
Where all things are endowed with magic life.
The sheltered birds are here more musical,
The little stream is edged with sweeter green,
The winds are balmier and of gentler motion,
The skies more bright, the season more propitious,
The trees of richer growth, and fruit and flower
Of fairer hue ; and here the human soul
Which bows in innocent love and worship finds
In joyous wonder more serene repose,
A calmer life, a nearer sense of heaven
Than elsewhere. King Lycander ! here confess
The power, the love, the mercy of the Goddess,
And bring a generous and repentant heart,
Fit offering to her shrine, and thou shalt have
Eternal freedom from thy torturing dreams,
And peace ineffable.

LYCANDER.

Seductive Spirit!
Speak on, speak on! There's music in thy words,
Which had those old astronomers but heard
Instead of that wild music of the spheres,
They ne'er had told its power, but died in silence,
Enamored of the sound. Tell me no more
Of Gods and Goddesses. Leave them to children,
Or those whom sickness or calamity
Makes childlike. Thou, sweet Agathe! to me
Art the sole genius of this happy place.
Could I transport thy subtle spirit now
To a bleak wilderness of Libyan sand,
Or the still region of eternal ice,
This radiant nature would spring up around thee,
Subservient and complete—the placid sky,
The lawn, the trees with ever-singing birds,
The sweet variety of hill and dale,
The golden beach, the shining sea, the temple—
And the first men who found the magic spot
Would kneel to thee, and call thee, chaste Diana!

AGATHE.

Forgive him, high-throned Goddess! O Lycander!

I shudder at this awful blasphemy.
Beware, O ingrate! lest Diana take
Her blessing from thee now. Must not the soul
Which makes its reckless mock of sacred things
Drink deeper guilt and with it deeper woe?
Think of the recent tortures of thy mind,
And of the peace and joy which banished them.
Beseech the Goddess, ever-merciful,
To let thy ravings pass unpunished by,
And dare no longer in her sanctuary
Make a vain idol of a mortal worm,
And question her supreme divinity.

LYCANDER.

Eloquently spoken, my sweet deliverer!
But all such lessons fall on heedless ears
In thy sweet presence. Hear me, Agathe!
Empire has lost its charm: the crown is only
A fiery circle on an idiot's brow,
Who bears its misery for its splendid show.
We will depart, we will abandon all—

AGATHE, (*weeping.*)

I never thought it would have come to this!
O Chrestus! Chrestus!

LYCANDER.

Love, my Agathe!
Will shortly dry thy tears; now listen to me.
There is an island of the Cyclades
Green to the water with perpetual verdure.
I passed it on my bounding way to Troy,
And my prow lingered, deaf to glory's call,
Within the blissful shadow of its hills.
It rose like Venus from the bright sea-foam,
An ever-shining jewel of the deep;
Too small for base ambition's selfish dream,
But large enough for love, whose happy kingdom
Is boundless. There eternal beauty reigns;
The very air is musical; the light
Lies lovingly upon the shadowy cliffs
And on the emerald sea; the woods are full
Of birdling voices prophesying love;
And canopies of purple cloud o'erhang
The far, enchanted valleys. It can woo
Soldiers from war and sailors from the wave,
Philosophers from academic shades,
Poets from fame and kings from ancient thrones,
All men from common duties, common pleasures,
To live entranced upon its flowery breast,

And all-forgetful of this human life,
Beneath Olympus find another heaven;
There will we dwell—

AGATHE.

No more, thou wicked King!
There let thy tongue be palsied: the deep curse
Is lowering o'er thee still. Hast thou forgotten
That I am Priestess of Diana's temple?
Does not her gift, a chaste, ethereal life,
Swell in my veins, and shall an earthly passion
Stain the pure current? Never, thoughtless
Monarch!
Cold as the moonbeam on the sleeping wave,
Cold as the new-fallen snow on Ida's top,
Purer than both, must be the vestal's heart
Who serves at great Diana's lustrous shrine!
Hence to thy crumbling palace! Thou hast breathed
Thy unchaste thought into my ear. Diana
Frowns on her silver throne; her dove of peace
Flies from thy breast forever. Leave the temple!

LYCANDER.

Nay, by the Gods thou fearest so, I will not!
Nor will I heed thy boasted sanctity,

The simple folly of an artless girl,
Enamored of religion's high romance,
And nurtured in the dim and solemn shade
Of this old temple. To the world with me!
Thou shalt be queen, yea, if thou wilt—a Goddess,
All men shall kiss thy feet. We will be happy—
Happier than those who live in highest heaven
And mock at human fate.

[*Embraces her.*

AGATHE.

Spare me, Lycander!
Diana! aid thy child!

LYCANDER.

When thus thou liest
In maiden trust and beauty on my bosom
Who—who shall pluck thee from my burning arms?
Which of the Gods?—

[*He pauses, slowly releases her and fixes his eye on vacancy.*]

Ha! thou detested phantom!
Dost come again? and this time with thy features
Convulsed with rage, no longer pitiful
With meek reproaches! I had thought thine image
Was blotted from the canvas of the mind.

Back to thy shades ! I laugh thee now to scorn !
I have protection from divinity.
Thou, Agathe ! can'st rid me of this fiend ;
One stately gesture of thy radiant hand
Will banish it forever.

AGATHE.

Ah ! I tremble
With sudden coldness, for the spiritual life
Which I receive from heaven has been withdrawn.
Quick from my presence, or I faint. Away !
Hence to thy punishment ! The Gods forsake
thee !

LYCANDER.

And thou—wilt thou forsake me, Agathe ?

AGATHE.

I can not help thee ; I have tried in vain,
Praying and weeping for thee ; now I fear thee,
And my whole soul by thy presumptuous sin
Is chilled with horror. Thy impurity
Is to my spirit like the loathsome air
Of dungeons.

LYCANDER.

Then I do resume my power;
And tell thee, sorceress! I am still a King.
Thou shalt become subservient to my wishes,
Or I will crush thee in this iron hand
As I would crush a flower.

AGATHE, (*Kneeling.*)

O great Diana, aid me!

LYCANDER.

Truce to thy prayers and listen to my words!
I will convey thee to a secret chamber
I know of in the temple. None will guess
Thy whereabouts, and clamor is in vain.
There will I leave thee to thy thoughts: there wait
Till midnight, when the moon has risen, my coming;
And when I come, be ready to my will,
Compliant as the shadow to the sun,
Or violence shall break what will not bend;
With this addition, that thy nearest friends,
Chrestus, thy sage old counselor and thy brothe ,
Shall hang as forfeit at my palace gate.
Headless to-morrow. Come, my beauty!

AGATHE.

Ah me!

Queen Goddess!—

[*She faints.*

LYCANDER.

Then I must bear thee hence. Delicious burden!
It would be sweet to kiss this snow-white brow,
And calm the pulses of this trembling heart,
If this were love's commotion, and not fear's—
She will recover soon—and then—at midnight!

[*Exit, bearing* AGATHE *out.*

SCENE III.

A CHAMBER IN THE PALACE.—LYCANDER ASLEEP ON A COUCH.

[*Enter* ELPENOR.

ELPENOR.

THIS royal house is tottering to its fall.
The guardsmen of its gate in conscious fear
Have all deserted it. Treason stalks in
And treads its silent chambers like a ghost
Unchallenged. Theron says 't is time to strike.

The plot of gentle Agathe has failed;
The King returned at sunset from the temple
Muttering and cursing as he came.
Good heavens!
Can a base fratricide forget his crimes,
And be refreshed with slumber? Ah, no! no!
I chid too soon the true, avenging fates:
'T is but the painful counterfeit of sleep;
He lies like one whose body is at rest,
But whose malignant and accursèd soul
Lurks in the face and struggles to betray
Its hideous workings. Lo! he stirs, he wakes;
'T is well, I would not strike him in his sleep—

LYCANDER, (*starting up.*)

Who talks of striking? Ha! thou coward Trojan!
Thrice have I chased thee round the walls to-day!
Now stand thy ground and let my thirsy steel
Drink up thy base-born blood—Ha! I was dreaming!
Slave! did'st thou speak of striking?

ELPENOR.

O Lycander!
I am Elpenor, come to claim my crown—

LYCANDER.

That name! that voice! Aha! I see! I see!
Thou hast at length cast off the crushing load
Of the great rock which bowed thy bleeding head.
Thou hast arisen! thou art alive, O brother!
And see! there is no blood upon thy face—
So youthful, happy, noble, bright in armor—
Why, it was all a dream! You are the King!
Years have not passed away. I am not old,
And gray and sorrow-stricken. I had a vision
Of a long war with Troy. Let me remember!

ELPENOR.

No trick, no subterfuge avails thee now;
My sword is consecrated to revenge:
Kneel and unbare thy bosom!

LYCANDER.

Softly, brother!
Speak not so fiercely: they will find us here;
Didst thou not hear a sound? Answer me truly!

ELPENOR.

The curtain rustled in a transient gust
That came through the open window.

LYCANDER.

'T was not that—
Not that—for it began last eve at sunset,
A faint and undistinguishable noise,
Less than the softest murmur of the sea;
But it increases, and it comes this way.
I know not why, a dreadful apprehension
Seizes me. Assure me that thou hearest it not!

ELPENOR.

Lycander! 't is the troubled phantasy
Of a spirit thoroughly diseased with guilt.
Why dost thou tremble so, and the big drops
Stand on thy brow? 'T is conscience tortures thee,
And conjures these illusions of the sense!

LYCANDER.

'T is no illusion, inexperienced boy!
I can interpret all, and yet I shudder
To think of it. Nothing have I seen as yet;
They are not visible, and yet I know—
From the dread palpitations on the air
I feel—that they are coming.

ELPENOR.

Who are coming?

LYCANDER.

Softly—the Furies! Ministers of vengeance!
Who else but they could thus unnerve me? Who
else?
Their imprecations load the trembling wind,
Their awful steps, not Jove himself can stay,
Cause the insensate earth to shudder. No altars
Are ever reared to them, no vows are paid them—
Deaf and implacable.—Elpenor! listen!
Can it be possible the bloody fiends
Give utterance to their thoughts in human speech?
Faintly but clearly canst thou not distinguish,
Amidst their unintelligible jargon,
My name, Lycander? It is! I hear it! They
come!
O whither shall I fly? Canst thou not save me?
[*Embraces* ELPENOR'S *knees*

ELPENOR.

I cannot kill this abject, grovelling wretch!
Unneeded sword! just Heaven has done thy work.
Revenge itself must turn to pity here

And weep at its own purposes. I came
Fully prepared, with every thought attuned
To be the minister of righteous vengeance,
But the dread powers of Pluto have forestalled me.
Shade of my father! from thy heavens look down
Upon this outcast, miserable man,
And pardon my relenting spirit. Here
Will I leave him to his punishment.

LYCANDER.

Leave me?
O leave me not! There, there, I hear them yet!
Silence is terrible; speak to me, stay with me,
Mock me, spurn me, curse me, strike me, kill me,
But leave me not! He goes!

[*Exit* ELPENOR.

O Jupiter!
Ruler of Gods and men, hear me but once!
If thou hast lightning in thine armory,
And mercy left to wing one flaming shaft,
Here let it fall!

[*Sinks to the floor.*

SCENE IV.

MIDNIGHT.—GROVE NEAR DIANA'S TEMPLE.

LYCANDER *alone.*

THE stars now keep their watches, and I mine;
They for the silent blessing of the world,
So Poets say—I for its malediction.
The excess of misery has made me calm.
The Furies pause, the phantoms disappear,
And strange serenity comes o'er my spirit,
Which, I am sure, presages nothing good.
'T is but the depth and silence of the river
Swift gliding on above the cataract,
Before its awful plunge. I feel impelled
By irresistible necessity
Headlong upon my fate. No thought of mercy,
No hope, no sweet compunction of remorse
Softens my heart. Lycander! promptly, boldly,
Improve this lucid moment: as the traveler,
Lost and benighted in the fearful woods,
Catches the lightning's flash to find his way,

Strike for thy life! My visitor was the son,
And in my fit I took him for his father.
He talked of vengeance, and he has good cause;
And when this young compassion has worn off
The spirit will return. Then, let it come!
Unconscious youth! thy movement should be
 speedy!
E'en while thou sleepest a spirit is abroad
Will do a deed which mars thy peace forever.
Treason, I think, is stirring in the wind.
Chrestus and Theron I so much distrust
That they shall die to-morrow. People mock me
Or think me mad; my crown has fallen to pieces,
My scepter glided from my careless hands.
The soldiery will hail Elpenor King
And hunt me, like a dragon, with their spears.
Gods! has it come to this? Down—choking wrath—
I would be luminously calm and cold
In this emergency. My cup of pleasure
Has not been emptied to the very dregs;
The last best drop is left. O, let me quaff it!
Another hour and Agathe shall fly,
A desecrated, melancholy thing,
Fit for the jeers and curses of the world.

Then will I seek Elpenor with this blade,
Which has been almost blackened in the blood
Of mighty heroes, and his shivering ghost
Hurl to the waiting shades. The spirit of
Troy
Is mantling o'er me ; I could fight my way
Through an embattled legion to my aim !

[*Exit.*

[*Enter* ELPENOR AND CHRESTUS

ELPENOR.

This way, good Chrestus ! I am sure I heard
Voices and footsteps here.

CHRESTUS.

Would it were he !
But do not strike or wound him, dear Elpenor !
Until the villain tells us where to find
Our Agathe. O Agathe ! my sweet !
My child, my Agathe !

ELPENOR.

O, it was strange
She was not in the temple ! I misgive—
I choke with apprehension—

CHRESTUS.

Quick on his traces!
He knows, or none. Ye Gods! O guide us now!
O Agathe! my child!

[*Exeunt.*

SCENE V.

SECRET CHAMBER IN THE TEMPLE.—AGATHE LYING ON A COUCH.

[*Enter* LYCANDER, *softly.*

LYCANDER.

Ye Gods! what envious and forestalling thief
Hath stolen into the garden of her body,
And plucked the rose of life?
Who comes behind me?

[ELPENOR AND CHRESTUS *rush in.*

ELPENOR.

Ha! Have I tracked thee to thy secret lair,
Thou royal wild beast?—Chrestus! what is this?
Agathe! asleep or dead? O Agathe!
Agathe, my sister!

LYCANDER.

Wake her if thou can'st.

ELPENOR.

Then hast thou killed her?

LYCANDER.

What and if I had,
Thou need'st not pluck thy fledgeling sword so quickly,
What if I had?

CHRESTUS.

She stirs, she lives, O see!

AGATHE.

What sound of angry voices has recalled me
Back to the world again? Such a sweet dream!
O do not wake me from this drowsy bliss.

ELPENOR.

O Agathe, my sister! wake and tell me
If this perfected villain hath yet wronged thee—

AGATHE.

O no! Diana was with me. I have escaped
His violence. Has the moon arisen, my brother!

ELPENOR.

Not yet, sweet sister! But the eastern stars
Stand all a-glow, in bright expectancy
Of her swift coming.

AGATHE.

Ah! when she has risen
And given Diana's blessing to the world,
Diana's virgin will have passed away
Into Elysium.

ELPENOR.

Alas! what does this mean?

AGATHE, (*to Chrestus.*)

Did'st thou not give me poison?

CHRESTUS.

And didst thou use it?
Why—it was meant for *him*. O Agathe!
O cursed foresight!

ELPENOR.

Chrestus! this from thee?
Fly, fly, old man! give her an antidote,
A speedy, wonder-working antidote!
Immediately! Old dotard! art thou palsied?

CHRESTUS.

Alas! there is no antidote.

ELPENOR.

Sayest thou so?
Then, by avenging heaven!—

AGATHE.

Elpenor, hold!
For shame! down—rather down upon thy knees,
Unthinking boy! and thank the kind old man
Whose wisdom saved us—me from worse than death—
Far worse! and thee from an eternal sorrow.

ELPENOR.

Alas! I see! I see!—

CHRESTUS.

Look, children, look!

What change hath come upon the fierce old king?
He kneels, he foams, the Gods have stricken him.

LYCANDER.

Hush! hush! I hear their footsteps in the hall.
Your voices will attract them hither—hush!

ELPENOR, (*stabbing him.*)

Hence to thy Furies, miscreant!

AGATHE.

Elpenor!
Thou strikest a madman! whom the Gods afflict
Mortals should spare.

ELPENOR.

No! let him die. The earth
Groans with his presence and the Furies seek him.

LYCANDER.

Not thou! poor stripling! but invisible powers
Have cut my life asunder. Thee I scorn!
I thought my blood was hot as living fire.
This blood—can it be mine? Ah! there they come,

The infernal sisters, changing men to stone
By a mere look! How horrible! My heart
Trembles with unimaginable terror!
Ward off, ward off the unutterable curse!
Their faces and their garments drip with blood;
The hissing snakes are wreathing on their heads;
They raise at once their scorpion lashes at me!
O aid me to my feet! O help me, shield me,
They strike, they strike, O mercy—mercy—
mercy—

[*Dies.*

CHRESTUS.

So terrible a death was never witnessed.

ELPENOR.

Fit termination to so foul a life!
But see, O see, his deadly work proceeds
To its sad consummation. Agathe!
O Agathe! my sweetest, dearest sister!
Look up, speak to me.

AGATHE.

Now the poison works!
Give me your hands—I can not see your eyes—

But well I know they are full of love and pity.
Grieve not, Elpenor! It is better thus!
The vestal fires pass from my hands undimmed,
The holy sanctuary undefiled!
I die, as I have lived, a spotless virgin.
Dear brother! if hereafter thou shouldst see
A lonely dove flit round the temple walls,
Give it my name and feed it for my sake.
A messenger it may be from the Gods
Presaging happiness to thee and thine.
Would I could kiss thy tears away, good Chrestus!
As I now kiss thy hand! Farewell! How strange!
How beautiful! The room is full of children;
The very air is full of infant faces,
So small, so bright, so beautiful, so many—
And see, Elpenor! Chrestus! see afar,
Before the crowded gateway of the stars,
Diana beckons me with shining hand;
Queen of the silver bow! I come—I come—

[*Dies*

[*Shouts and tumult without.*

[*Enter* THERON.

THERON.

Hail King Elpenor! The people crown thee
King!
Alas! What double tragedy is this?

ELPENOR.

Our tears inform thee better than our words.
Scepter and crown to-morrow! Thank the people,
Kind Theron, for me, and bear hence this corse.
Give it good burial for he was a King,
Although unworthy. Leave me then alone.
My thought, my heart, my life lies here to-night.
O bright, pure, beauteous, holy Agathe!

[*Exeunt all but* ELPENOR, *who kneels by the side of* AGATHE.

NOTES

TO THE POEMS.

I.

"ODE ON THE BIRTH OF A CHILD.

PAGE 13.

As this Ode is pervaded with the spirit of the New Church doctrine concerning Infants and Children, for its better understanding and appreciation I cite here a few passages from the writings of Swedenborg:

"That Infants are innocences is known: but that *their innocence flows in from the Lord* is not known. It flows in from the Lord because He is Innocence Itself, for nothing can flow in or be manifested in another except from some prior principle or cause, which is the thing itself.

"The Innocence of the Lord flows into the angels of the third heaven, where all are in the innocence of wisdom, and passes through the inferior heavens, but only through the innocences of the angels there, and thus immediately and mediately into infants: these are scarcely any thing at first but sculptile forms, receptible of life from the Lord through the heavens. But unless the parents also received that influx in their souls and in the inmosts of their minds, in vain would they be affected by the innocence of infants.—(*Conjugial Love*, 395, '6.)

"It has been told me from heaven that little children are especially under the Lord's auspices, and that there is an influx from the inmost heaven where the state of innocence prevails, which passes through their interiors, affecting them in its transit. It is from this source that innocence displays itself in their faces and in some of their gestures and becomes apparent, and it is this which so intimately affects their parents, and produces the peculiar emotion called parental love."—(*Heaven and Hell*, 277.)

"That the sphere of the love of infants is in like manner universal is manifest from that love in the heavens where there are infants from the earth, and from that love in the world with men, with beasts and birds, serpents and insects. Things analogous to this love are also manifested in the vegetable and mineral kingdoms; in the vegetable in that seeds are guarded with shells as with swathing-bands, and moreover are in the fruit as in a house, and are nourished with juice as with milk. That something like this is in minerals is manifest from the matrices and the cases in which the noble gems and metals are stored up and guarded.

"That innocence effects similar things with beasts and birds as with men is known. The reason that it produces similar effects is because *every thing which proceeds from the Lord in an instant pervades the universe.* And because it proceeds by discreet degrees and continual mediations, therefore it passes not only to animals, but even beyond, to vegetables and minerals. It passes even into the earth itself, which is the mother of all vegetables and minerals; for this in the time of Spring is in a state prepared for the reception of seeds as it were in the womb; and when it has received, it as it were conceives, cherishes them, carries in the womb, brings forth, suckles, nourishes, clothes, educates, guards, and as it were loves the progeny from them, and so on."—(*Conjugial Love*, 389–397.)

"What innocence is and what is its nature is known to few in the world, and not at all to those who are immersed in evil. It appears, indeed, before men's eyes, displaying itself in the face, speech and gestures, more especially of little children; but still what it consists in is not known, much less that it is the principle in which heaven inmostly abides with man."—(*Heaven and Hell*, 276.)

"Be it known, therefore, that every infant or little child, let him be born where he may, in the church or out of it, whether of pious or of wicked parents, is received by the Lord when he dies and is educated in heaven, where he is instructed according to Divine order, and is imbued with affections of good, and through them with knowledge of truth. Every person who thinks from reason may be aware that no one is born for hell, but all for heaven, and that if a man goes to hell the blame is his own, but that no blame can attach to infants or little children."—(*Heaven and Hell*, 329.)

"As soon as infants are resuscitated, which takes place immediately after their decease, they are carried up into heaven, and are committed to the care of angels of the female sex, who in the life of the body had been influenced by a tender love for little children and at the same time by love for God. As these angels had while in the world loved all infants with a tenderness like that of their mothers, they receive the little ones committed to their charge as if they were their own; and the infants on their part, from an inherent inclination, love them in return as their mothers. Every one has as many infants under her care as from spiritual maternal love she desires."—(*Heaven and Hell*, 332.)

"The state of infants in the other life far surpasses that of infants in the world, because they are not invested with a terrestrial body, but with one like those of the angels. The terrestrial body in itself is heavy or dull. It does not receive its first sensations and first motions from the interior or spiritual world, but from the exterior or natural, on which account infants in the world must learn to walk, to use their limbs and talk, and even the senses, as those of sight and hearing, must be opened in them by use. Not so in the other life. There, being spirits, they immediately begin to act according to their interiors. They walk without previous practice, and talk with the same readiness, only they speak at first from common or general affections, not yet perfectly distinguished into ideas of thought; but they are speedily initiated into these also, and the reason this is so easily effected is because their exteriors are homogeneous to the interiors."—(*Heaven and Hell*, 331.)

"It may seem a paradox, nevertheless it is most true, that the angels have a clearer and fuller understanding of the internal sense of the Word when it is read by little boys and girls than when it is read by grown-up persons who are not principled in faith grounded in charity. The reason is, as I have been informed, because little children are in a state of mutual love and innocence, consequently their receptive vessels are extremely tender and almost of a celestial nature, so as to be pure faculties of reception, which are therefore capable of being disposed by the Lord for the purpose, although this does not come to their consciousness, except by a certain sensation of delight suitable to their state and genius."—(*Arcana Cœlestia*, 1776.)

"So long as goodness and truth are possessed by man, whether it be in his childhood or in any other period of his life, evils and falsities can effect nothing; that is, evil spirits can not attempt to do any thing or to inject any evil. This is very evident in the case of infants, of well-disposed children and of simple-hearted persons, with whom although evil spirits or the very worst of the diabolical crew were present, still they could not affect any thing, but are kept in subjection. The reason why at this time they are in a state of subjection or servitude is, because man has not yet acquired to himself a sphere of lusts and falsities. For it is not allowed evil spirits and genii to operate, except on those things which man has actually procured to himself, not upon those which he receives hereditarily; wherefore before man procures to himself such spheres the evil spirits are in servitude, but as soon as ever he does, then the evil spirits infuse themselves into him and endeavor to obtain the dominion."—(*Arcana Cœlestia*, 1667.)

"That goodness is the principle which first of all is appropriated to man, is manifest from his infancy and early childhood; for it is well known that at that time he has the good of innocence and the good of love towards his parents and nurses, and the good of charity towards infant companions. *The good flows in from the Lord with infants, that it may serve in after years for the first principle of the*

Lord's life appertaining to man, and thereby for a plane to receive truths; this also is preserved with man when he grows up, if he does not destroy it by a life of evil and faith in the false thence derived."—(*Arcana Cœlestia*, 10-110.)

"In order to the better understanding of the nature of *remains*, let it be observed that they are not only the goods and truths which a man has learnt from his infancy, out of the Lord's Word, and which were thereby impressed on his memory, but they are likewise all *states* thence derived—as states of innocence from infancy—states of love towards parents, brothers, teachers and friends—states of charity towards the neighbor, and also of mercy towards the poor and needy; in a word, all states of goodness and truth. These states, with their goods and truths impressed on the memory, are called *remains*, which remains are preserved in man by the Lord, and are stored up, *unconsciously to himself*, in his internal man, and are carefully separated from the things of man's *proprium*, that is, from evils and falses. All these states are so preserved in man by the Lord that there is not the smallest of them lost."—(*Arcana Cœlestia*, 561.)

"Metals are equally significative with all other things in the Word. Gold in the Word signifies celestial good, which is inmost good. Hence it was that the ancients, who were skilled in the science of correspondences, called the ages after the metals. The first age they called the golden age because then reigned innocence and love and thence wisdom."—(*Apocalypse Explained*, 70.)

"Because these angels (those of the Golden Age, or Most Ancient Church) were of such a character, they dwell nearest to the Lord, from whom their innocence is derived; they also are separated from their *proprium*, so that they live as it were in the Lord. In outward form they appear simple and to the eyes of angels of the inferior heavens as little children, thus, as of small stature. They also appear not to possess much wisdom, though they are the wisest of the angels of heaven. These angels also are naked, because nakedness corresponds to innocence.—(*Heaven and Hell*, 280.)

II.

"OUR THREE CHILDREN."

PAGE 27.

"Our gold, our myrrh, our frankincense."

"BY gold, frankincense and myrrh are signified all things which relate to the good of love and faith in the Lord; by gold the things which are of the good of love, by frankincense the things which are of the good of faith, and by myrrh the things which are of each in externals. The reason why the wise ones from the East offered those things was, because amongst some of the orientals from ancient times there remained the science and wisdom of the ancients, which consisted in knowing and seeing celestial and divine things in those things which are in the world and upon the earth. For it was a thing known to the ancients that all natural things corresponded to spiritual things, and were representative and thus significative, as is also evident from the most ancient books and monuments of the Gentiles. Hence it was that they knew that gold, frankincense and myrrh signified the goods (good affections and thoughts) which were to be offered to God."—(*Swedenborg's Arcana Cœlestia*, 92, 93.)

III.

"CHILDHOOD."

PAGE 31.

"THERE are certain societies of Angels, and those many in number, which have the care of infants. They are chiefly of the female sex, consisting of such as in the life of the body have had the most tender love towards infants. These angelic spirits discoursed moreover concerning infants on earth, declaring that immediately on their nativity there are angels attendant on them from the heaven of innocence, and in the succeeding age angels from the heaven of the tranquility of peace, afterwards angels from the societies of charity, and next other angels in proportion as innocence and charity decrease with the infant children, and lastly, when they become more adult and enter into a life alienated from charity, angels indeed are present, but more remotely, and this according to the ends of life which the angels direct by continually insinuating good ends and averting evil ones; and in proportion as they are able or unable to affect this, their influx is nearer or more remote."—(*Swedenborg's Arcana Cœlestia*, 2,302, 3.)

IV.

"THE CHILD AND THE RIVULET."

PAGE 51.

"THAT there is a relation to man in all things of the created universe, may indeed be known from what has been adduced, but can only be seen obscurely; whereas in the spiritual world it is seen clearly. In that world also there are all things of the three kingdoms, in the midst of which is the angel, who sees them about him, and knows that they are representations of himself; yea, when the inmost principle of his understanding is opened he knows himself and sees his image in them as in a glass."—(*Swedenborg's Divine Love and Wisdom*, 63.)

V.

"TO A ROSE."

PAGE 66.

"Heaven, in the Word in its internal sense, does not signify the heaven or sky which is apparent to the eyes of the body, but the kingdom of the Lord universally and particularly. He who looks at things internal from those that are external, when he views the heavens or sky, does not think at all of the starry heaven but of the angelic heaven. When he beholds the sun, he does not think of the sun, but of the Lord as the sun of heaven. So when he sees the moon and the stars also, yea, when he beholds the immensity of the heavens he does not think of material immensity, but of the immense and infinite power of the Lord; so also in other instances, since there is nothing but what is representative. He likewise regards earthly objects in the same view. Thus, when he beholds the first dawn of the morning light, he does not think of the day-dawn, but of the rise of all things from the Lord, and their progression to the full day of wisdom. In like manner when he looks on gardens, shrubberies, and beds of flowers, his eye is not confined to any particular tree, its blossom, leaf or fruit, but he is led to a contemplation of the celestial things represented by them, neither does he behold only the flowers, their beauties and elegancies, but is led also to regard the things which they represent in the other life; for there is not a single object existing in the sky or in the earth which is beautiful and agreeable, but what is in some way representative of the Lord's kingdom."—(*Arcana Cœlestia*, 1,807.)

"I have discoursed with the angels concerning representatives, observing to them that in the vegetable kingdom on earth there is nothing but what in some measure represents the kingdom of the Lord. They replied that every thing in the vegetable kingdom which is beautiful and ornamental derives its origin through heaven from the Lord, and that when the celestial and spiritual things of the Lord flow into nature, such objects of beauty and ornament are actually created, and that thence proceeds the vegetative soul or life. Hence also come representatives, but this, being unknown in the world, was called a heavenly arcanum."—(*Arcana Cœlestia*, 1,632.)

VI.

"THE WILD RE-UNION."

PAGE 86.

THIS Poem, which may appear strange or mystical to some readers, is designed to illustrate the impossibility of divorcing the Good from the True. The union of the Good and True is the *heavenly marriage* so frequently mentioned by Swedenborg, and so constantly alluded to in the internal sense of the Bible. It is indeed by the unition of the Will-principle or living element with the Understanding-principle or thinking element that every useful or practical effect is brought about either in the spiritual or natural worlds. The essential point in regeneration is the coöperation of the Understanding illuminated by Divine Wisdom, a light with the Will actuated or impelled by Divine Love or heat. The same heavenly marriage is represented by the union of Father and Son—by the mystical love of the Lord and his Church—and universally by the conjugal relation, in which woman represents the Will and man the Understanding.

Every thought, or truth which is an object of thought, has a corresponding emotional state of the soul or love, created with and organically attached to it. We are "saved by faith," because the truths of the Word stored up in the mind call down from heaven their corresponding good states of the life, which we generalize as the Christian graces and virtues.

The masculine and feminine elements of the conjugial love experience super-eminently this organic attraction after an eternal unition. Separated forcibly for awhile by evil influences, the emotional element is represented in the poem as reappearing in its body, which it reanimates simply to serve as a medium for bringing it into contact with its corresponding intellectual principle. Contact having been effected, spiritual attraction prevails over mere chemical affinity, and the spirits are supposed to ascend to heaven together.

VII.

"BEAUTIFUL! DIVINELY GLOWING."

PAGE 118.

"Us who are no longer twain."

"SINCE the inhabitants of heaven are from the human race, consequently the angels who occupy it are of both sexes; and since it was ordained from the creation that the woman should be for the man, and the man for the woman, thus that the one should be the other's, and since the love that it should be so is innate in both, it follows that there are marriages in the heavens as well as on earth. Marriages in the heavens, however, greatly differ from the marriages on earth."

"In the heavens, marriage is the conjunction of two into one mind; the nature of which conjunction shall be first explained. The mind consists of two parts, one of which is called the understanding, the other the will. When those two parts act in unity, they are then called one mind. In heaven the husband acts as that part called the understanding, and the wife as that which is called the will. When this conjunction which exists in the interior descends into the inferior parts which belong to the body, it is perceived and felt as love, and the love thus felt is *conjugial* love. This is termed in heaven dwelling together, and it is said of such that they are not two but one. Therefore in heaven two married partners are not called two, but one angel," (moreover they actually appear to others at a distance as in one body, and they enjoy a continued sensation themselves of the oneness or identity of their bodies.) "That there should exist such a conjunction of the husband and wife in their inmost parts, which belongs to their minds, results from creation itself." (In other words, souls are created as sexual pairs, and the relation of husband and wife is organic and eternal.)—See *Heaven and Hell*, 366, 7, 8, and the succeeding paragraphs on Marriages in Heaven.)

VIII.

"ORLEANNA."

PAGE 121.

"We shall meet and love in heaven."

"*That the Lord provides similitudes for those who desire love truly conjugial, and that, if they are not given in the earth he provides them in the heavens.* The cause is this, that all marriages truly conjugial are provided of the Lord; but in what manner they are provided in the heavens I have heard described by the angels, thus: That the Divine Providence of the Lord is most particular and most universal concerning marriages and in marriages, because all the enjoyments of heaven stream forth from the enjoyments of conjugial love, as sweet waters from the stream of a fountain, and that on this account it is provided that conjugial pairs be born, and that these are continually educated under the auspices of the Lord for their several marriages, both the boy and the girl being ignorant of it, and after the completed time, that marriageable virgin and young man meet somewhere as by fate and see each other; (if not on earth surely in the other life), and that there, as from a certain instinct, they instantly know that they are partners, and as if from a certain dictate within think in themselves, the young man that she is mine, and the virgin that he is mine, and after this has been seated for some time in the minds of both, they deliberately speak to each other and betroth themselves. It is said, as if from fate's instinct and dictate, and it is meant from divine providence because whilst this latter is not known it appears thus: for the Lord opens internal similitudes that they may see each other."—(*Conjugial Love*, 229.)

IX.

"MYSTIC UNION"

PAGE 185.

This Poem refers to the New Church doctrine of regeneration; but as the subject is metaphysical in its nature, I have here given the truth but a poor and inadequate expression. The following brief explication will perhaps enable the reader to see the Poem in a better light.

The "dead" are the spiritually dead, even while living in the natural world. The "resurrection," or progress from death unto life—in other words, regeneration, takes place by union with the Divine Humanity of our Lord. Jehovah, the Father, or Divine Love, took on himself a weak and infirm human nature derived from the Virgin Mary—subject to all of our trials and temptations, yet without sin. This human nature is called Christ, or the Son of God. Thus the "beautiful Ideal" becomes incarnate in the "grosser Real." Christ purifies and elevates this infirm human nature, "the Father working in him"—making it fully Divine, "re-molding it by patterns from above." We are to "follow him in the regeneration;" as the Father worked through him so he is to work through us. In other words he gives us a new internal or spiritual man, and we are to bring our external or natural life into strict accordance and correspondence with it—so that it shall resemble the mystic union of soul and body. This labor of regeneration is represented by the six days of creation followed by the "Sabbath" of victory and repose. "Heaven and earth" represent our inner and outer, or spiritual and natural life thus brought into operative harmony.

X.

"DESCENSUS AVERNI."

PAGE 198.

THIS Poem is written in accordance with the science of correspondence, and conveys spiritual instruction through the medium of natural imagery. The subject is the origin of evil, or the fall from heaven, and involves the same spiritual truths which are concealed in the narrative of Eve's temptation and the expulsion from the garden of Eden. I will recapitulate them in condensed form, referring the inquisitive reader to the first volume of Swedenborg's *Arcana Cœlestia* for a luminous exposition of this most difficult question in Revealed Religion.

The essential feature in the process here described is the passage of the soul from a spiritual into a natural state of life—which is a descent from an interior or higher to an exterior or lower plane of thought and affection. To make this more clear we must briefly define the difference between the spiritual and the natural man.

The spiritual man occupies an interior stand-point, and he thinks of nature from the Lord as a fixed center. Nature is to him a grand panorama or mirror wherein are objectively seen represented the myriads of spiritual things which belong to the Lord's kingdom. This is the condition of the angels in heaven, and was also the first state of men upon earth. By becoming natural or external men they fell. The natural man occupies an exterior stand-point and views the Lord and all things of his spiritual kingdom from Nature as a fixed center, consequently either not at all or in great obscurity. He interprets every thing in a sensuous manner, and finally ends in believing nothing which he can not see, hear, taste or handle, and make the subject of physical experiment or analysis. Indeed, so spiritually blinded does he become that in his infatuation he calls this gross naturalism the highest wisdom. He can not conceive that the human mind was ever constituted so differently as precisely to reverse his favorite mode of philosophizing, and at last any thing like spiritual thought he denounces as mysticism.

How did man fall from the lofty state of intuition or spiritual perception of truth? By listening to the seductions of the senses. The evidence of the senses, unenlightened by a higher spiritual and revealed philosophy, which explains the senses themselves, must lead entirely astray. Many things *appear* to the senses to be true which are only apparently true, and the great mass of truths never appear to the senses at all. The sun *appears* to revolve around the earth but does not; the heavens above *appear* to terminate in a blue vault but do not. Objects *appear* to be in rapid motion and we ourselves *appear* to be stationary, when the very reverse may be the case. Sensation *appears* to reside in the surface of our bodies, but its real seat is far within; much deeper indeed than the natural body itself. Our thoughts *appear* to originate spontaneously with ourselves, yet they have come to us always by influx from angels and spirits. Our life *appears* to be our own, inherent with and inseparable from our organization, and yet the Lord alone has life and we are merely recipient vessels or organs of life. Man by thinking naturally or sensuously divorces his mind from faith in God and from insight into spiritual things, and finally natural appetites supercede spiritual aspirations, and from being merely *sensuous* in thought he becomes *sensual* in life.

In the Poem before us, as in every jot and tittle of the Biblical narrative of the fall, these great truths are typified. The youth wandering from the "holy meridian" of heaven down to its crystalline borders, represents the Understanding gradually receding from the interior to the exterior stand-point above specified, as from the center to the circumference of a circle. It is then that it begins to doubt and ponder upon the "awful riddle of life." In this state heavenly things (and the Lord in them) which have been received implicitly and perfectly into childlike affections, become to be made the matters of intellectual investigation. In hieroglyphic language, the sun "dwindles to a star," charity is becoming mere faith.

Pursuing its researches into the outermost or natural sphere of life, the Understanding yields itself up to the guidance of the senses. The serpent in all ancient writings, hieroglyphic, mythical or correspondential, represents our sensuous sphere of thought, or the mode of philosophyzing from the evidence of the senses. This serpent tells us that it is not God's life but our own life which animates us, and we forthwith "become as gods" in our own eyes, and begin a life separate from God. His leading the Youth to a fountain of water wherein he has injected his poison, indicates that the Understanding becomes deceived by the appeal which the senses make to merely natural or apparent truth, water representing that truth. The interference of the Dove represents the effort of some remains of innocence with its intuitional light to reject the subtle sophistries of the senses. The change in his external world is representative of the difference between thinking spiritually and thinking naturally. The change first happens in his mind, and then by correspondence in the things which appear around him. The "crystalline walls" have become a mere "iron door," and "the cataract of God's Light is changed to "a region of stone-heaps and shadows." Doubt, darkness, confusion have succeeded to the order and beauty of angelic life and the light of angelic wisdom.

XI.

"THE MAGIC GARDEN.

PAGE 202.

THIS Poem and the "Descensus Averni" were written to illustrate the most ancient style of composition in the world, viz., by correspondences. Natural objects, whether singly or in groups, various and shifting scenery and transformations, even the historical development of facts, may be used as the mediums or vehicles for spiritual thought. This interior thought is not visible on the surface, and is only brought out by the proper key, namely, a knowledge of the science of correspondences. The whole Bible was written on this principle, and Swedenborg has not invented but re-discovered the key which was lost. One familiar with Swedenborg's expositions will see the meaning of this Poem almost at a glance, but for those to whom the whole principle is still an unrevealed secret, I here append a brief statement of the internal or spiritual sense.

VERSE 1ST.—There is a spiritual state of mind based upon good affections, and elevated far above the sensuous sphere, concealed from the uninitiated or merely natural man by a cloud or veil of literal appearances. "Garden" throughout the Bible represents a state of intelligence and wisdom. The "air" indicates its spirituality or elevation. Upheld by "mountains," signifies based upon affection; the "mountain of the Lord" means a state of lofty and sublime love to God. "Clouds" invest or envelop interior things—as the letter of the Word does its internal. Our Lord's coming in "the clouds of heaven" at the latter day means that he will elucidate the true meaning of the letter by the descent and manifestation of the internal sense or spiritual signification from within. These meanings are not arbitrary but fixed and eternal.

VERSE 2D.—In that state of spiritual intelligence we perceive that what we call Nature or the outward world is always merely phenomenal and representative of interior things, and not actually causative or existing of itself.

VERSES 3D AND 4TH.—The only real and eternal things are *the organic forms* of the soul and their infinitely varying states, which by peculiar spiritual laws are scenically projected or made to appear as it were out of the mind and independent of it. This objective world is the image of the subjective one, every natural object in it representing and being caused by some spiritual form or essence in the mind.

VERSE 5TH.—When in this elevated sphere of thought we ponder upon the great question of Duty, the "sacred enigma" why we are here, and what we are to do? we are instructed from within by symbolic scenes having a most beautiful and apparently independent externeity or outness.

VERSE 6TH.—Our unregenerate ruling love or passion appears to us in the most enchanting form. Woman always represents the affectional element.

VERSES 7TH AND 8TH.—The unregenerate Understanding or Intellect recognizes as exceedingly beautiful and fascinating that form of evil affection which corresponds to itself, and which it surveys from its own false stand-point.

VERSES 9TH AND 10TH.—This love of self and the world would teach us that it is right and the dictate of heaven for us to be guided by our own natural instincts and passional attractions, and its influx produces in the sphere of consciousness the most disorderly emotions, which must terminate in sorrow and shame, although pronounced supremely delightful by the unregenerate mind.

VERSE 11TH.—Every thing beautiful to the eye or fragrant to the sense is the outbirth of some good affection flowing from the Lord and received into the souls of angels or men.

VERSE 12TH.—The Church of the Lord, or the organic embodiment of Good and Truth, so as to be presented to the intellectual consciousness, (in the individual soul represented by love to the Lord and the neighbor) appears under the form of a beautiful virgin.

VERSE 13TH.—She offers for our spiritual reception and appreciation the pure truths of the Word, the simple and precious treasures of Revelation, unfalsified by love of self and the world.

VERSE 14TH.—This is the true and living water, that blessed spiritual truth which inculcates that conjoined exercise of faith and charity which is the *heavenly marriage* productive of eternal peace.

VERSE 15TH.—The False springing from the evil detests the Truth which emanates from the Good. Truth feels only a tender compassion for the False.

VERSE 16TH.—The Church of the Lord is our *spiritual mother*, who nourishes us with her sacred truths and draws us into a life of cheerful obedience by gently leading our affections.

VERSE 17TH.—We are enlightened by the spiritual truths of the Church to perceive that the love of self and the world is really a despicable, miserable creature, which, under a false show of superior pleasure, is actually tortured by the lusts of the senses.

VERSE 18TH.—And that said self love is the deeply hidden cause of all the hideous or poisonous objects in nature, which are created as its outbirths, and correspond to all its evil and selfish passions.

VERSE 19TH.—The spiritual truths thus acquired are fixed among the constellations of the inner or heavenly mind, and when we descend to our natural sphere of life again, our hearts are in that state of love to the Lord and the neighbor which is represented by praying with our faces towards the East. "Stars" in the Bible always mean spiritual truths or knowledges of interior things. The "stars falling from heaven" mean the loss of spiritual intelligence by the Church, &c. The East where the sun rises, in the supreme sense means the Lord himself: in a secondary or proximate sense, it signifies that heavenly frame of mind in which we are receptive of his divine life in our hearts: hence the ancient temples all pointed towards the East, and praying with the face towards the East was a general custom derived from correspondence, and perpetuated long after the worshippers had lost a clear perception of its original significance.

XII.

"SPIRITUAL VISION.

PAGE 207.

THIS Poem is based upon one of the most beautiful laws of the spiritual world, viz., that the objective scenery surrounding a spirit is not fixed as it is in the material world, but plastic, and the changes which it undergoes are representative of the subjective changes occurring in the mind of the spirit. To illustrate this more plainly, I make an extract from Swedenborg, for which, although treating of a delicate subject, I offer no apology, since it is not only artistically beautiful but pregnant with a moral lesson greatly needed in this degenerate age:

"I heard a certain spirit, a young man fresh from the world, boasting himself of his scortations, and among the insolences of his boasting, he gave vent also to this, 'What is more doleful than to imprison one's love, and to live alone with one woman? And what is more delightful than to set the love at liberty? Do not those things which are obtained by cunning, deceit and furtive arts delight the inmosts of the mind?' On hearing these things the by-standers said, Do not speak thus; you know not where you are, and with whom you are; you have but lately come hither: hell is under your feet and over your head is heaven. You are now in the world which is mediate between these two, and is called the world of spirits. Here arrive and here are collected all who depart from the world, and here they are explored as to their quality, and the evil are prepared for hell and the good for heaven. Perhaps also you were taught by preachings in the world, that whoremongers and harlots are cast down into hell, and that chaste consorts are elevated into heaven. At this the new comer laughed, saying, 'What is heaven and what is hell? Is not heaven where one is free? And is not he free who is permitted to love as many as he likes? And is it not hell where one is a slave? And is he not a slave who is obliged to adhere to one?' But a certain angel looking down from heaven heard this, and broke off the discourse, lest it should proceed further towards profaning marriages, and he said to him, Ascend hither and I will show to the life what heaven is and what hell is, and of what quality the latter is to confirmed scortators. He showed the way and he ascended. After reception he was led first into a paradisal garden where were fruit trees and flowers, which, from their beauty, pleasantness and fragrance filled the mind with the utmost delight; which, when he saw, he admired with great admiration, but he was then in external sight, such as he was in in the world, and in this sight he was rational, but in internal sight, in which scortation took the lead and occupied every point of thought, he was not rational. For that reason his external sight was shut and his internal sight was opened; which, being opened, he exclaimed, What do I now see? Is not this straw and dry wood? And what do I now perceive? are they not stinking things? Where are now the paradisal things? The angel answered; They are near and they are present, but they do not appear before your internal sight which is scortatory, for this turns heavenly things into infernal and sees nothing but opposites. Every man has an internal mind and an external mind, thus internal sight and external sight. With the evil, the internal mind is insane, but the external is wise; but with the good the internal is wise and from this the external also: and *as the mind is, so man in the spiritual world sees objects.*

"After this, the angel, from power given him, shut up the man's internal sight and opened his external sight, and conducted him where he saw magnificent palaces of alabaster, marble, and various precious stones, and beside them porticoes, and round about columns overlaid and surrounded with stupendous ornaments and decorations. When he saw these things, he was amazed and said, What do I see? I see magnificent things in the utmost magnificence, and architectural things in their very art—but at that moment the angel shut up his external sight and opened the internal, which was evil, because filthy; which being done, he exclaimed, saying, What do I now see? Where am I? Where are now the palaces and magnificent things? I see nothing but heaps of rubbish and cavernous places. But presently he was brought back into external sight, and introduced into one of the palaces, and saw the decorations of the gates, of the windows, of the walls and of the ceilings, and especially of the utensils, upon which and around which were heavenly forms of gold and precious stones, which can not be described by any words, nor delineated by any art, for they were above the ideas of language, and above the conceptions of art. On seeing these things he again exclaimed, These are more marvellous things than the eye has ever seen. But at this moment his internal sight was opened, his external sight being shut as before, and he was then asked what he saw. Nothing, he answered, but walls, here of bulrushes, there of straw, and in another place of burnt sticks.

"But yet again he was brought into an external state of mind, and virgins were presented to him who were beauties because images of heavenly affections, and they addressed him with the sweet voice of their affection; and at that moment from seeing and hearing them his face was changed and he returned of himself into his internals, which were scortatory; and because such internals can not endure any thing of heavenly love, and on the other hand can not be endured by heavenly love, both parties vanished, the virgins from the sight of the man, and the man from the sight of the virgins. After this the angel instructed him whence were the inversions of the states of his sight, saying, I perceive that in the world from which you have come you were double, one man in externals and another in internals; that in externals you were a civil, moral and rational man, but in your internals the reverse, because a whoremonger and an adulterer, and such, when they are permitted to ascend into heaven and are there held in their externals can see the heavenly things therein, but when their internals are opened, in place of heavenly things they see infernal ones. Know that, with every one here the externals are successively closed and the internals opened, and thus they are prepared for heaven or hell. And because the evil of scortation defiles the internals of the mind above every other evil, it is not possible that you should not be carried down to the filthy things of your love, and these things are in hell. After hearing this he descended and returned into the world of spirits and to his former companions, to whom he spoke modestly and chastely but still not long."—(*Conjugial Love*, 477.)

XIII.

"THE SHEPHERD OF CYPRUS."

PAGE 210.

THIS Poem is written according to the Science of Correspondences, and involves spiritual truths in its interior signification.

The general truth taught is this—that the human soul in childhood or a state of infancy is conjoined with the celestial heavens, and receives influx from thence, which by a powerful, subordinating control over all natural passions prepares it for a life on earth of great usefulness and for heaven hereafter.

The boy represents the human mind as to the understanding or intellectual principle: the girl represents the will or emotional principle. Their tending sheep together at the foot of the mountain represents their harmony in a state of natural goodness. The number of sheep, twenty-four, twelve to each, represents the fullness or completeness of that innocent state. Thus prepared for the revelation and reception of interior or spiritual goodness, they cross the stream, which, like the Jordan or river of death, represents the boundary line between the natural and spiritual.

Their being attracted to the mountain summit by invisible music represents that no didactic or philosophic impression is made upon the tender mind at this stage, but it is operated upon through its affections—music representing those interior emotions which can not be analyzed. The tender, loving impulses which come over them as they ascend the mountain, represent the increasing influx of divine and angelic love into the soul, corresponding to its spiritual ascent or elevation towards the celestial sphere. St. John, the Apostle of Love, appears to them, representing conjunction with and perception of the celestial heavens. Children on earth in the innocence of ignorance really receive interior lessons and suggestions of celestial love from angels who like John have attained to the innocence of wisdom.

The soul now quickened and enlightened by such intercourse with the highest heavens, descends again to the cares and duties of life. The Lamb accompanying the will principle represents the state of innocence which is derived from the Lord. The eagle accompanying the intellectual principle, represents the strength and clearness of the understanding in its perception of spiritual truth. The lion and serpent being harmless and asleep, represent that the natural passions and thoughts are entirely subordinated to the spiritual passions and thoughts of a soul which is truly regenerated, or in heavenly order.

On crossing the magic line, spiritual things disappear from natural sight; but the effect is now visible in the natural sphere. The little girl dies, or is elevated to the celestial angels as John predicted, and the boy becomes a disciple of John, and finally an Apostle of Truth. In other words, the will principle is truly and fully elevated into heaven, or sanctified whilst the understanding becomes thereafter a better and fitter medium and minister of divine truth.

The wild beasts by which the holy old man is devoured represents that gross, wicked and sensual character of mind which not only fails to appreciate, but ignores, hates and would always destroy every manifestation of divine truth. Greek and Roman Philosophy was of this sensuous and naturalistic type, and waged incessant war against Christian spirituality, but was extinguished by the more vital power.

XIV.

"THE GRAVEYARD."

PAGE 232.

"The grandsire, from his honored bier,
Rose up to share immortal youth."

"THEY who dwell in heaven are continually advancing towards the vernal season of life, and the more thousands of years they live there, the more delightful and happy is the state of Spring to which they attain, and this goes on to eternity with continual increments, according to the progressions and degrees of their love, charity and faith. Those of the female sex who had died old women, quite worn out with age, but who had lived in faith in the Lord, in charity toward the neighbor, and in happy conjugial love with their husband, come more and more in the course of years into the flower of youth, accompanied with such beauty as surpasses every idea of beauty perceptible to the sight. In one word, in heaven to grow old is to grow young."—(*Heaven and Hell*, 414.)

XV.

"NEW THANATOPSIS."

PAGE 235.

I FIND the relations between the spiritual and natural body of man so lucidly described in a little New Church Tract on "Death and the Resurrection," (Philadelphia Series, No. 3), that I will avail myself of some of its paragraphs to give the reader a clearer insight into the philosophic and religious teachings of the Poem.

"There is an outer world and an inner; in the one every thing, even the least, is material: in the other every thing, even the least, is of spiritual substance. These two worlds are the creation of the infinite and eternal Jehovah. He has created them from his Divine love by means of his Divine wisdom, and these two essentials of his Divine nature are united in every thing which exists from him, whether in the natural world or in the spiritual. Whatever, then, of the Good and True is the object of our senses in the material world must be regarded as the Divine love and wisdom in their ultimate effect; and whatever of like character exists in the spiritual world, as these same Divine principles in their higher, purer and more perfect degrees of manifestation. These two worlds are most intimately related, even as soul and body in man. For as the body is dependent on the soul or spirit for all it has of life, motion and use, so is the material world dependent on the spiritual world within for all it possesses of beauty, form, motion, harmony and use. They stand related to each other therefore as cause and effect. Indeed all the phenomena of this natural world are so many effects or combinations of effects, the ends and causes of which must be sought in the spiritual world. There is not a single thing in any one of its three kingdoms, mineral, vegetable or animal, which does not derive its origin from the spiritual world.

"The sun with his heat, light and other imponderable agents, together with the atmosphere, waters, and all things else existing and subsisting from him, are so many *out forms* (or outbirths) of elements and principles existing in the spiritual world, and, in the language of the New Church, are called *correspondences* of those things which are their prototypes in that world. This material world, therefore, considered as a whole, is but one grand symbol of a still more perfect, beautiful, and glorious world within, and every part, even in its least, is a correspondence of something existing in that world. But a truth which we should most carefully keep before our minds while considering this subject, is that while these worlds are thus intimately related the one to the other, they are yet most distinct from each other; for what is material can have nothing in common with what is spiritual. Each substance has its own proper laws, and they can no more commingle than the thoughts and affections of the mind can chemically combine with the fibers composing the head and face of the human body. But while thus distinct, these two worlds are most intimately conjoined by means of the *laws of correspondence*, so as to constitute in the eye of him that made them but one world.

"Every created being commences the career of his existence in the material world, the lowest sphere of creation. Divine order requires this, for there is no angel, much less any evil spirit, created such. But every inhabitant of the spiritual world, whether good or evil, whether an angel of the highest heaven or spirit of the lowest hell, was once an inhabitant of some material earth, and what he is now is the orderly consequence of what he was while in that state. The order of man's progression is from external things to internal, from natural things to spiritual, from earth to heaven.

"Hence it is that man is endowed with a twofold nature; one constituting him an inhabitant of the natural world, the other of the spiritual at one and the same time. And he possesses the senses, organs and faculties both mental and bodily, which are adapted to these two modes of existence. He possesses a material body and mental faculties connected with it, which adapt him to this world and its uses, and within the material a spiritual body with mental faculties which adapt him to the spiritual world and its uses. This inner or spiritual body, like the outer or material, is human in form. It is indeed the man himself; for it is the form of his mind, and hence the dwelling-place of his thoughts and affections, the *subject* of all consciousness, the seat of the memory, and of every other mental faculty. In fine, all that he has thought and willed, said, learned and done, enjoyed and suffered, is treasured up within this form—inscribed upon it in characters which are indelible. The material body in the view of the New Church is in itself *dead*, destitute alike of motion and sensation, the passive instrument of the spiritual body within, the medium through which that body holds communion with the natural world, and acts and performs uses in that world. It is the spiritual not the material body which really sees and hears, feels, tastes and touches. The material body is but a tissue of fibers, so organized as to permit the spiritual to receive these impressions from the outer world.

"With these consideratiens in view, we may understand something of the nature of death and the resurrection, or how man is removed to the spiritual world. Death is but the withdrawal of the spiritual form from the material, with which it is clothed while in this world. When the material body is no longer capable of serving the spiritual as a medium between it and this world, or when the material has fully served its function in gathering up from this world all that can ever be useful to the indwelling spiritual, then it is cast off and dies, falls back again into the lowest kingdom of the material world, becomes subject once more to the chemical and physical laws of that world, is resolved back into the ultimate elements and particles of which it is built up, and thus enters into the composition of other material forms.

"But the spiritual body rises into the world proper to it, and which is its true and eternal home. All of man that can die is the material body; but he himself can never die. What is commonly called death is only the passage of man from one world to another. It is simply a fact, or as it may be termed, a single point in the orderly process of the spirit's development; a process as strictly in accordance with the laws of Divine order as that by which the caterpillar is changed into the butterfly. The caterpillar contains within itself the butterfly, which may at any time be disengaged by dissection. While the caterpillar is feeding upon the food proper to it, and developing itself, the butterfly is also developing itself, and when the caterpillar dies, immediately breaks forth from its chrysalid prison-house, and enters upon a new and higher mode of existence, feeding upon finer, choicer, more exquisite food than before, and entering on new and higher uses and delights. But this analogy fails in one very important particular, which is, that while the butterfly, like the caterpillar in which it is for the time enveloped, is *material*, with man, on the contrary, the outer form alone is material, the inner being spiritual, and having nothing in common with material substance.

"The New Church teaches that man, after having left this world and entered upon the life of the spirit, never returns to take upon himself a material body; for this would be as directly opposed to the order of things as for the butterfly, after sporting in the balmy air of Spring, and roaming through fields of flowers and sweets, to turn back in its course, and creep into the hard, horny case which nurtured and protected it in its chrysalid state, or for an eagle, after soaring into the empyrean and drinking in the rays of the sun, to return to the nest which cradled his infancy, and attempt to clothe himself in the shell from which he was hatched."

"That when a man passes from the natural into the spiritual world, as he does when he dies, he takes with him all things belonging to him as a man except his terrestrial body, has been proved to me by manifold experience. For when he enters the spiritual world or life after death, he is in a body as he was in the world; to all appearance there is no difference whatever, because there is none that he can discover either by touch or sight. But his body is now spiritual in its nature and thus separated or purified from the terrestrial particles; and when what is spiritual touches and sees what is spiritual, the effect to the sense is exactly the same as when what is natural touches and sees what is natural. The man when a spirit enjoys every sense, both internal and external, that he possessed in the world. He sees as before, he hears and speaks as before, he smells also and tastes, and feels when he is touched as before, he longs also, he desires, he wishes, he thinks, he reflects, he is affected, he loves, he wills as before, and a person who takes pleasure in study reads and writes as before. In a word, a man's transit from one life into the other or from one world into the other is like a journey from one place into another, and he takes with him all things that he possesses within himself as a man; so that it can not be said that a man after death, his death being only that of his terrestrial body, has lost any thing that belonged to himself. He also carries with him his natural memory, for every thing that he ever heard, saw, read, learned or thought, from his earliest infancy to the last day of his life he still retains. The natural objects, however, which are contained in his memory, not being capable of being reproduced in the spiritual world, remain quiescent, just as they do with a man in the world when he does not think of them; but, notwithstanding, they are reproduced when the Lord sees good."—(*Swedenborg's Heaven and Hell*, 461.)

"In what manner resuscitation is effected, has not only been related to me, but has been shown to me by actual experience. I was myself made the subject of that experience, in order that I might fully know how the great change is accomplished.

"I was brought into a state of insensibility as to the bodily senses, and thus nearly into the state of dying persons, the interior life nevertheless remaining entire, together with the faculty of thought, that I might observe and retain in my memory the particulars of the process I was about to undergo, being such as is experienced by those who are being resuscitated from the dead. I perceived that the respiration of the body was almost taken away, the interior respiration which is that of the spirit remaining, conjoined with a slight and tacit respiration of the body.

"There was opened, in the first place, a communication with the Lord's celestial kingdom as to the pulsation of the heart, because that kingdom corresponds to the heart in man. Angels belonging to that kingdom were also seen, some at a distance and two sitting near my head. By their means all affection proper to myself was taken away, but thought and perception still continued. I was in this state for some hours. The spirits who were around me then withdrew, supposing I was dead. There was also perceived an aromatic odor like that of an embalmed corpse; for when celestial angels are present, the effluvium of the corpse is perceived as an aromatic perfume, on smelling which, spirits are unable to approach. By this means also evil spirits are driven away from the spirit of a man when he is first introduced into eternal life. The angels who sat at my head did not speak, but only communicated their thoughts with mine. When their thoughts thus communicated are received, the angels know that the man's spirit is in such a state as to be capable of being drawn out of the body. The communication of their thoughts was effected by directing the aspect of their countenances on mine; for it is by this means that communications of thought are produced in heaven.

"As thought and perception remained with me, in order that I might know and remember how resuscitation is accomplished, I perceived that those angels first examined what my thoughts were, to see if they were similar to those of dying persons, which are usually engaged about eternal life, and that they wished to keep my mind occupied with such thoughts. It was told me afterwards that a man's spirit is kept in the last thoughts which he had whilst his body was expiring, till he returns to the thoughts which flow from the general or governing affection which had possessed him in the world. It was particularly given me to perceive and to feel also, that there was a drawing and as it were a pulling out of the interiors belonging to my mind, thus of my spirit, from the body; and it was told me that this proceeded from the Lord, and that it is this which effects the resurrection.

"The celestial angels who thus minister to the resuscitated person do not leave him, because they love every one; but if the spirit is such in quality that he can not longer continue in company with celestial angels, he feels a desire to depart from them. When he does so, angels of the Lord's spiritual kingdom come to him, by whom the use of light is given, for previously he saw nothing but only exercised his thoughts. It was also shown me how this is done. Those angels seem to unroll as it were the coat of the left eye towards the nose, that the eye might be opened, and the faculty of sight imparted. It appears to the spirits as if such an operation were actually performed; but is only an appearance (significative of some spiritual process). After the coat of the eye has thus seemed to be drawn off, a lucid but indistinct appearance is observed, like that which on first awaking from sleep, a man sees through his eyelids before he opens them. This indistinct lucid appearance as seen by me was of a sky-blue color, but I was afterwards informed that there are varieties in the color as seen by different persons. After this there is a sensation as if something were gently drawn off the face, and when this operation is completed, the resuscitated person is introduced into a state of spiritual thought. That drawing off of something from the face is likewise, however, only an appearance, and by it is represented the passing from a state of natural thought into a state of spiritual thought. The angels use the utmost caution lest any idea should proceed from the resuscitated person but such as partakes of love. All this being done, they tell him that now he is a spirit.

"After the spiritual angels have imparted to the new-born spirit the use of light, they render him all the kind offices which in that state he can possibly desire, and instruct him respecting the things which exist in another life, so far as he is capable of comprehending them. But if the resuscitated person is of such character as not to be willing to receive instruction, he desires to withdraw from the company of those angels. The angels, notwithstanding, do not leave him, but he separates himself from their society; for the angels love every one, and desire nothing more than to perform kind offices to all, to give them instruction, and to take them to heaven, in which consists their supreme delight. When the spirit has thus separated himself from the society of the angels, he is taken charge of by good spirits, who, whilst he remains in their company, also do him all sorts of kind offices. If, however, his life in the world has been of such nature that he can not abide in the company of the good, he also desires to be away from them. This conduct he repeats during a longer or shorter period of time, and in fewer or more instances, till he becomes associated with such spirits as completely agree with his life in the world. In their company he finds his own life, and what is wonderful, he then pursues a similar course of life to that he had led in the world.

"I have conversed with some on the third day after their decease, when the process had been completed that is described above. Three of these had been known to be in the world, to whom I related that preparations were now being made for the burial of their body. I happened to say for their burial, on hearing which they were struck with a sort of stupor, and declared that they were alive, but that their friends might commit to the grave what had served them for a body in the world. They afterwards wondered exceedingly that when they lived in the body they did not believe there was such a life after death, and they were especially astonished that within the Church almost all are possessed by a similar incredulity."—(*Heaven and Hell*, 448–58.)

www.ingramcontent.com/pod-product-compliance
Lightning Source LLC
LaVergne TN
LVHW010148110826
845151LV00002B/454

* 9 7 8 1 4 2 5 5 3 7 7 6 0 *